The Hammermill Guide to
Desktop Publishing in Business

The Hammermill Guide to Desktop Publishing in Business

Bruce G. McKenzie

Hammermill Papers
Memphis, Tennessee 38197

Library of Congress Cataloging in Publication Data

McKenzie, Bruce G., 1946–

   The Hammermill guide to desktop publishing in business.

   Includes bibliographical references

      1. Desktop publishing 2. Business literature — Publishing —
Data processing 3. Business — Data processing I. Title

Z286.D47M379   1989   686.2'2544536   89-85645

ISBN 0-9615651-X

Hammermill Papers Business, International Paper Company,
6400 Poplar Avenue, Memphis, TN 38197

Civilization advances by extending the number of important operations which we can perform without thinking about them.

— Alfred North Whitehead

Of all horned cattle, the most helpless in a printing-office is a college graduate.

— Horace Greeley

Contents

Foreword

By Jeffrey F. Kass, Vice President, Hammermill Papers

The purpose of this book is to help people look good on paper.

The people we have in mind

- own, or are thinking of getting, a desktop publishing system

- work in organizations whose main business is not "publishing"

- hold jobs as administrators, managers, marketers, engineers, researchers — just about any job where skill in graphic design and typography isn't in the job description

Our premise is that as soon as you take up desktop publishing, you're *doing* graphic design and typography. You're involved in the graphic arts.

Welcome to the business.

This is not a computer book. As papermakers, we at Hammermill applaud the proliferation of computer books and manuals. May it flourish forever. But there's no reason for us to add to it.

We *do* have a legitimate interest, however, in helping people get the most satisfaction out of using our paper. To produce professional-looking publications takes — besides great paper — some understanding of the conventions of "publishing." Typographic and graphic design conventions of today have evolved through zillions of pages over 500 years; their value to printed messages in the competition for readers' attention is proven. In this book we have tried to set forth in a useful way the considerations of typography, graphics, and design that are most important in making publications clear, orderly, effective, classy, and business-like.

We also think it likely that most people involved with type and graphics via desktop publishing will sooner or later get involved in high-volume electronic or offset printing. As a leading supplier of printing, laser, and copier papers, we know a lot about those areas, so we included a chapter on graphic arts production. And, because there is a natural connection between desktop publishing and desktop presentations (and because our papers are so well suited to the many handouts associated with the latter), there's a chapter on desktop presentations.

Once people have gone to the trouble of creating a professional-looking publication, no matter how simple its layout or mundane its purpose, naturally they're going to want to print it on high-quality paper. That's the easiest way to add class. There's a lot in this book about paper. Certainly more than any computer book you're likely to pick up!

Finally, since this a book intended for people in business, we asked David Shay of KPMG Peat Marwick to contribute a management perspective on desktop publishing. His *Afterword* describes *Eight Ways to Cost-Justify Desktop Publishing*.

We hope you find *The Hammermill Guide to Desktop Publishing in Business* interesting and useful.

Preface

To me, the most essential and amazing thing about desktop publishing is that anyone can produce pages in the office that look as if a commercial printer printed them. How Benjamin Franklin would envy us! We can do with a few keystrokes what the printers of his day took infinite pains to do. Even so, with their klunky equipment and laborious methods, our printing forebears could undoubtedly do better work, faster, than most of us starting out in desktop publishing — for this reason: *they knew the rules*. That's what this book is mostly about.

Businesspeople take up desktop publishing because they want to produce professional-looking publications. And they can. But here's the catch: every graphic arts professional since Gutenberg has learned structures and usages which stand in the same relationship to the printed word as grammar does to language. Graphics, contrasting type styles, rule lines, white space, and the other tools of the page designer determine the sense of words and ideas, much as do word order and sentence structure. As with grammar, so with page layout and typography: you can get away with flouting or ignoring convention, but not without risking misunderstanding and losing credibility.

Thus, the main objective of this book is to give a clear account of professional publishing practices likely to be useful to people in business. In addition, for readers who are just thinking about getting started with desktop publishing, the first chapter sketches what you need to know about the technology. Readers who have yet to allocate a DTP budget, and readers who have responsibility for managing a DTP function, should find the *Afterword* by Dave Shay of KPMG Peat Marwick particularly valuable.

Many people helped make this book.

At Hammermill, Ken Walsh, Randy Akers, Jack Willow, Tom Harvey, Jerry Vrabel, John Gorski, Keith Steele, Rose Marie Kenny, and Rod Hardinger brought support, vision, and knowledge to the project. No surprises there: this team helped develop the first laser papers specifically for desktop publishing.

Several of our (Business Information Graphics) clients — Paul Verga at Metropolitan Life, Bob Soudant at NYNEX, Joe Acevedo at Standard and Poor's/McGraw Hill, and Tom Powers at Chemical Bank — read drafts and, as is the custom of clients, made forceful comments which greatly improved the finished product.

Frank Romano, editor/publisher of *TypeWorld*, corrected errors and contributed new information as well as encouragement.

John Giles of the National Association of Quick Printers, Linda Clayton of Ginny's Printing & Copying (Austin, Texas) and Carl Gardner of the University Hills PrintShop (Denver) explained quick printing. Earl Headad at Landart Systems, Inc., a New York service bureau, helped set up the photograph on page 125. Andy Plata and Skip Henk at COPI (Houston), Susan Brodsky at ProTypography (Chicago), and Howard Greenberg at Axiom Design Systems (New York) provided insight on imagesetting and the services available at service bureaus. Axiom did the imagesetting for the book. Tony Oppenheim, a New York consultant, served as computer wizard. Anthony Melidy of Kerningware (Toronto) answered many questions about DTP fonts.

Commercial printers who gave freely of their time and knowledge are: Darrel Dundore at D. L. Terwilliger (New York), Sherman Sussman at Tanagraphics (New York), Jack Schultz at Dispatch Printing (Erie, Pennsylvania), and Lee Daniels and Shelly Wermes at Daniels Printing Company (Boston). Daniels printed the book.

My associates at Business Information Graphics shaped this book into what you're looking at. Lorna Pautzke edited, rewrote, prodded, managed production, checked facts, found or cooked up many of the examples. Ilene Korey Price art-directed and designed the book, and created many illustrations. Other illustrations were drawn by Tony Coccia, who also designed the cover and divider pages. Kim Rendleman researched and drafted the sections about paper and served as editorial consultant. Sheree Reinbach did the legwork on rights and permissions.

Even with all this help, errors undoubtedly remain which are, obviously, mine. Knowing that desktop publishing is one of the fastest-evolving components of the information age, and hoping the book proves a useful enough tool to warrant a revised edition, we encourage readers to send suggestions and comments to: Guide to Desktop Publishing, Hammermill Papers, 6400 Poplar Avenue, Memphis, TN 38197.

Bruce G. McKenzie
New York, August 1989

The Hammermill Guide to Desktop Publishing in Business

1

Essentials

1.1 What Is Desktop Publishing?

Desktop publishing brings the power of the printed word — the impact and clarity of type and graphics — to anyone with access to a personal computer.

Definition

The phrase *desktop publishing* (DTP) denotes the production of typeset documents using small computers. The essential idea is that a person without special training, operating a microcomputer, does the work of typesetter, artist, and page makeup department in composing typeset pages of text and graphics. He or she then either prints the pages (at a rate of about eight per minute) on a desktop laser printer, or, if the job is beyond the capacity of a desktop printer, sends the computer files to an outside service for conventional processing and printing.

Desktop publishing caught on fast, is expected to grow fast (chart), and has propagated fast: desktop presentations, animations, business forms, videos, comic books, multi-media extravaganzas . . . the list of desktop activities gets longer every day.

Forecasted Unit Sales of Page Layout Software
1987–1992

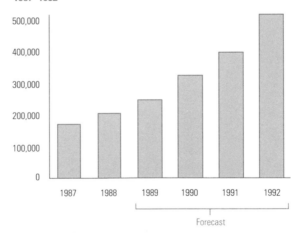

Source: *Computer Publishing Systems* — BIS CAP International, Inc., January 1989.

The prime mover in the spread of these activities is the ease with which text can be typeset and printed. Typeset text, particularly combined with graphics, has impact and perceived quality. People prefer it because it's easy to read. Never before has it been easy to produce.

There are many advantages to desktop publishing.

- It can save time and money over conventional graphic arts processes.

- What you see — on the screen or the laser printout — is what you get: revisions can be made at once and often, at little or no cost.

- Computers used for desktop publishing are almost always easy-to-use computers with graphical interfaces.

- Microcomputers purchased for desktop publishing can carry out many other tasks, such as database management, word processing, and telecommunications.

- Nearly all computers used for desktop publishing are connected to some sort of network; many are connected to worldwide electronic services.

- People *enjoy* producing higher-quality work.

Whatever the reasons for purchasing a desktop publishing system, people find uses for it they hadn't anticipated. They also find that DTP is not as effortless as it looks in the computer-makers' advertising.

Desktop publishing demands computer competence, graphic arts skills, and intellectual effort. The purpose of this book is to provide some of the know-how needed to make the effort more productive.

1.2 Hardware

The basic equipment for desktop publishing is a personal computer linked to a laser printer. The hardware is compact and uncomplicated, though profoundly sophisticated. Additional devices like film recorders and scanners multiply the options.

Computers

A desktop computer consists of the following:

• *Keyboard and mouse*

The keyboard and mouse (pointing device) together make up a graphic interface which enables the user to edit text and move objects about on the screen in an intuitive, natural way.

• *Central processing unit (CPU)*

The heart of the computer is its central processing unit. The CPU is a microprocessor, a powerful integrated circuit that carries out instructions given in electronic form. The information processed is *digital* information.

• *Read-only memory (ROM)*

ROM contains routines (programs) for the essential operations of the computer itself and some repetitive processing operations like mathematics.

• *Random access memory (RAM)*

RAM is where the computer stores volatile information as it is being used. Desktop publishing requires more RAM than standard applications like word processing.

• *Storage devices*

The storage medium may be small *floppy* magnetic disks, a large permanent *hard disk*, magnetic tape, or a compact laser disk (CD). A disk or tape *drive* retrieves, stores, and updates the electronic information. High-capacity storage (20+ megabytes) is required for desktop publishing.

• *Monitors*

The monitor screen displays information for the user. Like a television tube, a monitor is an electron gun firing at a screen covered with phosphors.

The ideal monitor for desktop publishing would be a perfect, high-resolution image of a page as it will appear when printed. This is an impracticable ideal in desktop systems — for one thing, monitors must operate much faster than printers, redrawing the screen continuously; consequently, they operate at lower resolution.

Computer platforms

Two computer *platforms,* IBM and Apple Macintosh, using different operating systems, dominate desktop publishing. In addition, some powerful minicomputer workstations are specifi-cally designed for publishing. Costs of computer processing have decreased, and demands made on desktop machines have in-creased, to the point where desktop machines and minicomputer workstations are converging.

Many desktop publishing application programs are available in versions compatible with several operating systems and are designed to make it possible to work on the same document from any platform. Certainly, good (and bad) quality is attainable from any platform.

Laser printers

RASTER
RASTER
RASTER
RASTER
RASTER
RASTER
RASTER
RASTER
RASTER
RASTER
RASTER

Raster image processing uses a laser to expose the drum, one line at a time, moving across and down the page like a raster scan of a television screen. This process is used in many computer-controlled devices besides printers.

Laser printers and photocopiers work by xerography ("dry-writing"). The heart of a xerographic printer is a selenium-coated drum. Selenium has the peculiar property that when it is exposed to light, it loses electrical resistance to the point where it cannot hold an electrostatic charge. In a xerographic printer, the drum is given a *uniform* electrical charge, in the dark, by the *corona* wire.

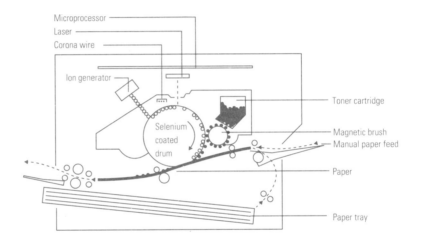

The drum is then exposed *selectively* to light.

- In a *photocopier*, the light is reflected onto the drum from the image being copied; only the non-dark areas of the original reflect light to the drum.

- In a *laser printer*, the light comes from a laser beam or laser diode controlled by a microprocessor. The controller, according to instructions from the software being used, turns the light on/off at the rate of 300 times per inch of travel across the drum. This is the printer's *resolution*: 300 dots (or "spots") per inch. Devices that work in this fashion are called *raster devices* and the controllers are called *raster image processors* (RIPs). Higher resolutions are, of course, possible — it's necessary only to turn the beam on/off more frequently. But that takes significantly more processing and more computer memory, which is why high-resolution printers cost more and work so much more slowly than desktop laser printers.

Where light strikes the laser printer's drum, the electrostatic charge dissipates. After this selective discharging, the drum rotates through a cloud of charged toner particles (plastic ink powder). The particles collect on the electrically charged areas to form a printing image; they fall away from places that have been discharged. The rotating cylinder finally fuses the image to paper by heat and pressure.

Other output devices

• *Film recorders*

Film recorders convert page descriptions onto film, commonly as 35mm slides. Film recording uses a process similar to laser printing, except that the beam of light exposes film instead of a drum. The light passes color filters, as instructed by the computer, before reaching the film. Some film recorders require special font wheels for high-resolution text: in these, text is imaged one character at a time by light passing through a film disk spinning in front of the light source.

• *Color printers*

Inkjet and *wax thermal* transfer printers use a process similar to that used in laser printers to create type and graphics with a raster image processor. Wax thermal transfer printers use special films impregnated with colored wax to transfer the image to paper. Inkjet printers spray colored ink through tiny nozzles. While no color *laser* printer is currently on the market for desktop publishing, such printers, using technology similar to that used in color copiers, will doubtless become available.

Film recorder

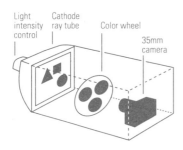

Inkjet printer

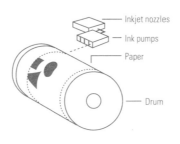

Wax thermal printer

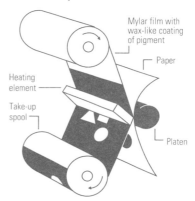

- *Imagesetters*

Imagesetters use raster image processing to expose photo-graphic paper or film at resolutions from 900 dots per inch to over 3000 dots per inch. The exposed material is developed by photo processing. Many desktop publishers refer to high-resolution imagesetting as "typesetting," because the high-resolution type output is like that of professional photographic typesetters. However, since the imagesetter outputs both type and graphics, *imagesetting* is the more descriptive term.

- *Digital printing press*

This emerging technology combines imagesetting and offset printing. An image carrier (*plate*) is created on the press for each of the colors and black. The image area of the plate is ink receptive; the non-image areas are not. The result is process color printing.

Digital Printing Press Schematic

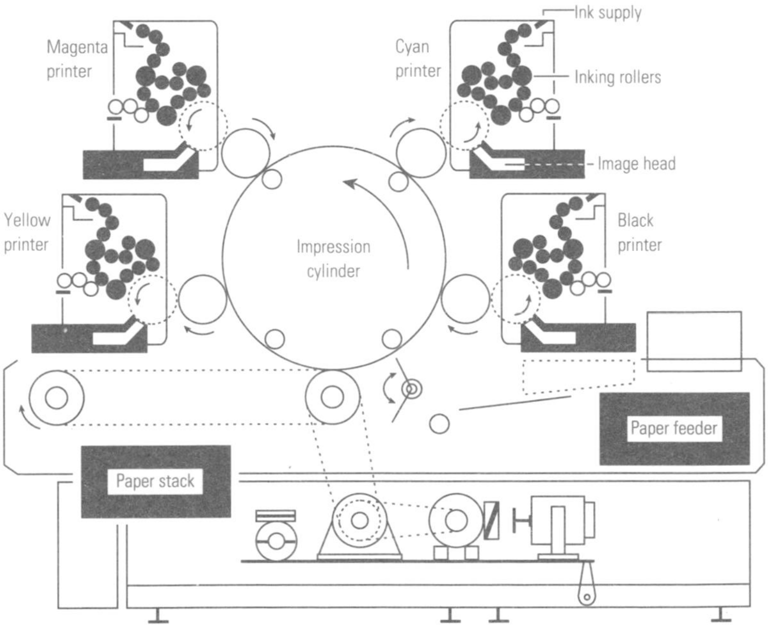

Dots, spots, and resolution

Dots per inch (dpi) is the standard way of classifying image quality of output devices.

This measurement refers to dots per *linear* inch, not per *square* inch. Thus, the resolution of a 600 dpi printer is actually *four times* that of a 300 dpi printer (36,000 dots per *square* inch versus 9,000). Because most imaging devices use standardized software, it is possible to print the same computer file on many different printers or imagesetters. Graphic arts quality is said to begin at 1000 dpi. Office printers are typically at 300 dpi. It has been suggested that *spots per inch* (spi) would be a better term for the resolution of raster devices, because it distinguishes printer dots (the smallest marks a printer can make) from the *halftone* dots used to specify the resolution of photographs (halftones) in conventional printing. It takes an arrangement of about 10 printer spots to make the equivalent of a halftone dot. The table below shows typical applications for devices at low, medium, and high resolution.

Low resolution	Medium resolution	High resolution
(300–400 spi; halftone equivalent 30–40 dpi)	(600–900 spi; halftone equivalent 60–90 dpi)	(1270–2540+ spi; halftone equivalent 120–250+ dpi)
Office work	Manuals	Color
Proofing	Directories	Advertising
Newpapers	Forms	Promotion
Demand publishing	Magazines (B&W)	Annual reports
	Books	
	Journals	

Source: *Typeworld*, April 1988.

Other input devices

Images and text for desktop publishing need not be created at the keyboard or drawn with the mouse. Digital information useful in desktop publishing can be generated by a number of devices.

- *Scanners*

Essentially a photocopier for a computer, a scanner translates pictures into computer information. A *scanner* performs in reverse the functions of a print engine: it converts light reflected from a page into a digital description of the page. This image can be further interpreted (as text, for example) and refined by specialized software.

- *Digitizing tablets*

A digitizing tablet is an electronic drawing tablet which records the movements of a hand-held electronic stylus as it draws or traces graphics.

- *Digitizing recorders*

Computer-generated desktop presentations may benefit from sound captured by computer recording devices.

- *Television/VCR*

Computers can be equipped with special circuit boards to enable them to read and store video signals.

- *Fax*

Computers can be equipped to send and receive data from facsimile machines, so that a "picture" of a page can be sent to a fax machine without printing out the page, and a person without a fax machine can receive an image that can be printed on a laser printer.

Networks

Sharing computer files on networks makes it easier to get things done. The prevalent form of networking in offices is sometimes called "sneaker-net" — walking a floppy disk from one computer to another. If the computers are of different types, *file conversion* is required. Depending on the computers and software involved, the difficulty of changing files from one format to another varies from none-at-all to not-worth-the-trouble.

File conversion and sharing is much easier over a local area network (LAN) — computers physically connected to one another and various other devices by cable or wire. Most desktop publishing in business takes place in the context of a LAN sharing a common printer. LANs can be networked to other LANs, to mainframes or minicomputers, or to wide area networks (WANs) over telephone lines. WANs are commercial database and E-mail (electronic mail) services which offer storage and forwarding of computer files to other subscribers, along with a vast array of transaction and information services, such as on-line banking, access to financial or scientific databases, and airline reservations.

Modems

Modems connect computers to telephone lines. They convert (MOdulate) computer data into signals that can travel over telephone circuits, and they convert (DEModulate) such pulses received from other computers. Computer connections via modem are *dial-up* connections. The exchange of information is much slower than it is over LANs. But modems are very useful for searching commercial databases, exchanging files, and for electronic mail. Desktop publishers often use modem connections to send files to service bureaus for high-resolution imagesetting.

1.3 Software

This section outlines concepts common to all software used in desktop publishing and describes the types of application programs likely to be needed by desktop publishers in business.

Software fundamentals

The ability to set type and lay out pages requires little or no computer knowledge, certainly no knowledge of computer languages or programming.

Nevertheless, when computers fail to do what they're "told," the frustrating task of figuring out how to rephrase the instructions can sometimes be speeded up by recalling how fundamentally unimaginative computers are.

Bits, bytes, and text

Computers are *digital* devices which respond only to streams of bits and bytes. A *bit* is a unit of voltage ("on" or "off"), a unit of information in the computer's memory circuits. Bits are represented by the binary number system, in which the only integers are 1 and 0 (1=on, 0=off). A *byte* is a collection of 8 bits, which, taken together, can produce up to 256 different patterns, representing the integers from 0–255, for example.

These integers, in turn, can stand for other things, such as the letters of the alphabet. For example, in the American Standard Code for Information Interchange (ASCII, pronounced "ass kee"), the letter *A* is represented by the pattern 01000001, which corresponds to the integer 65. ASCII coding is used for the transmission of simple text data. Files used in desktop publishing can be thought of as containing text (ASCII codes) and formatting information, like different type styles or spacing arrangements. No matter what program was used to create the file, the text can generally be extracted and used separately. This is often done in moving information from one program to another, from a database to a word processing program, for example.

It is not practical for human beings to write complex commands in ones and zeroes ("machine language") or other integers, so collections of commands are assembled into general-purpose *languages,* such as BASIC, PASCAL, "C", and special-purpose languages, such as the page description languages used by laser printers.

Page description and printing

• *Page description languages*

Each type of printout device operates under its own language, called a *page description language* (PDL). This is a set of codes that enable the printer to perform its functions, such as centering copy, changing type size, advancing paper, and positioning graphics. After a page is assembled on a *front end* system — the computer connected to the printer, for example — the screen image is translated into the printer's language via a program called a *printing driver.* In changing from one type of printer to another, one must change printing drivers.

The PDL interprets the code from the driver, combines it with font information from other sources, and assembles everything for the raster image processor (RIP). The RIP converts the page description to an electronic grid — a map with one bit of information for every printer spot to appear on the final page (a *bit-map*). The RIP sends a stream of bits to the *marking engine,* which actually puts the spots on the paper or film.

PDLs are largely standardized so that a variety of printout devices can accept the same information and print it at resolutions ranging from 300 dpi to 2540 dpi. PostScript from Adobe Systems is a leading standard PDL.

Though efficient, this approach to printing requires considerable computer power. A large part of the cost of laser printing is attributable to the cost of the page description language software.

• *Fonts*

Fonts (typefaces) used in desktop publishing are themselves computer programs, collections of equations describing the outlines of the characters which make up the font, drawn at small size, to be scaled up as required by the PDL. Each font program contains resources needed to draw the letterforms on the relatively low-resolution monitor (screen font) and resources for high-resolution printers (printer font). Printer fonts may reside in the printer's memory or in another computer, from which they are sent to the printer (*downloaded*) as needed.

In calculating letterforms, each line segment or curve marked off requires its own computer calculation.

 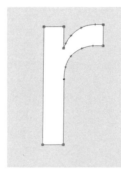 

Times Roman   Helvetica   Charter

The user interface

A major advantage of electronic publishing is the visibility and interactivity of the page being worked on. The operator can see all typographic and layout changes immediately on the screen. Unfortunately, there is no single word meaning "the interactive integration of text and graphics" — *publishing* is often used as a synonym.

Interactive commands are based on the use of *menus* listing the typographic and functional alternatives available. The user defines, with an electronic pointer, the text or graphics he or she wants to change. That item is then highlighted on the screen. The proper menu is chosen and the individual function within it selected. The highlighted material is then changed, and the result is immediately displayed on the screen. It is common to see both menu-driven and keyboard-coded approaches used within the same system or program. For instance, the change to bold type could be made via the menu or by keying ***B**. Almost all systems include the ability to see type and graphics on screen in simulated page form with all items in position.

Interactivity of computer screen and printed page is the key to ease-of-use in desktop publishing. Illustrated here are screens and resultant pages created with two of the most popular DTP programs, Aldus Corporation's PageMaker (running on an Apple Macintosh, showing pulldown menus) and Xerox Ventura Publisher (running on an IBM PC).

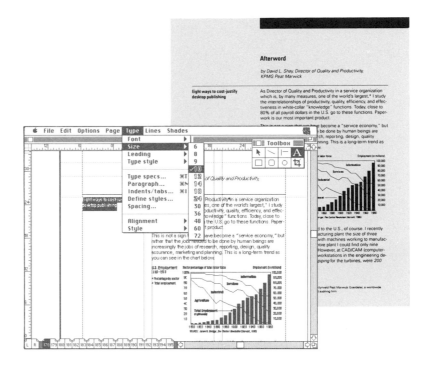

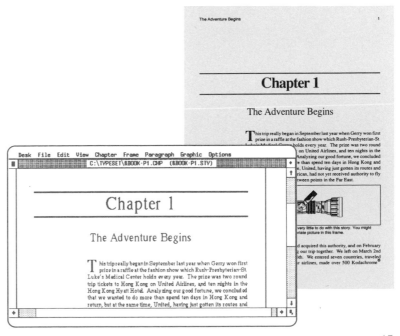

Application programs

Programmers compile sets of instructions written in programming languages into *application programs* for word processing, for graphics, for page layout, and so forth. With these application programs, computer users create *files* or *documents*. Files can easily be read and modified by the application programs that created them. Many application programs can convert files to or from other applications' formats. It is also common to extract text only (using ASCII codes) from word processing, spreadsheet, and database files to be used with other applications.

Following are the types of application programs most commonly used in desktop publishing:

• *Text (word) processing*

Word processing programs are designed to manipulate and format text. Some have graphics capabilities; some generate desktop presentations. Outlining programs, too, are text processors (see §2.2).

• *Graphics/drawing*

Some graphics programs create simple bit-mapped pictures with resolution equal to that of the screen. (Each screen dot becomes a printer dot.) These are called *paint* programs. More sophisticated programs combine powerful *drawing* routines for curves, outlines and other forms. These programs use all the capabilities of higher-resolution output devices like laser printers. They may allow the user to tint, rotate, distort, shade, and blend images, and to create gradients and other special effects. Some graphics programs are designed for specific purposes, such as creating graphs, architectural drawing, or 3-D modeling. The most powerful of these graphics programs are classified as CAD (computer-aided design) programs.

• *Page layout*

Page layout programs are used to integrate text and graphics, both usually created by other applications. All these programs have drawing and text-handling capabilities built in.

• *Spreadsheets/databases*

These programs are intended primarily for data management and calculation. Many have graphics capabilities such as charting, and options for creating forms such as invoices or price lists.

• *Desktop presentations*

These are hybrid programs that combine text processing, layout, outlining, drawing and other tasks required in creating slides, overheads, and on-screen presentations.

• *Forms design*

These applications also combine the features of layout programs, such as drawing rules and shapes, with calculation and data management. Some allow the user to scan in an existing form, then modify it to suit his or her needs.

• *Communications*

Transmitting data over telephone lines requires translating computer data into audio signals and back again, and establishing *protocols* for sending, receiving, and checking whether transmission has been successful. Telecommunications programs (sometimes called *terminal emulation* programs) dial phones, make connections, and control data translation and file transfer.

• *Scanning*

Optical character recognition (OCR) software interprets the shapes in scanned pages as *text*, turning the pages into word processing files. Though accuracy is not perfect, this kind of scanning can save a great deal of typing. Other scanning software digitizes scanned images for manipulation as graphics.

2

Layout and Typography

2.1 Elements of a Page

The beginning of wisdom, Confucius said, is to call things by their right names. Knowing what to call the parts of the page makes it easier to figure out where to put them.

Margins: half of the page

The *margin* is what isolates text and graphics from the outside environment. About half the area of the page should be left for margins. (Standard margins for 8½-by-11 pages conform to this rule; see diagram below.) The part of the page used for text and graphics is the *live area*.

The top margin is measured from the top of the page to the top of the first line of type in the live area. Text (e.g., chapter titles, page numbers) within the top margin is called a *header* or *running head*. The bottom margin is the space from the bottom edge of the page to the bottom of the last line of type in the live area. Type inside the bottom margin is called a *footer* or *running footer*.

Standard margins on 8½-by-11 paper result in 48 square inches (6 x 8) of live area and 45½ square inches of margin (2½ x 11) + (3 x 6).

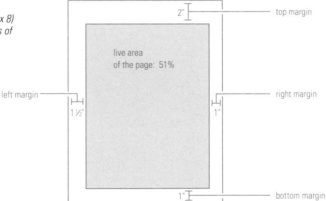

Margins contribute to readability.

Along with other areas of white space on the page, margins contribute to the readability and the attractiveness of a publication. The more white space, the more refined the publication looks. Art books and annual reports use a very generous amount of white space.

Gutters; odd and even pages

Publications printed on both sides of the page follow conventions which make life easier for readers and publishers alike.

Gutter: space for binding

- It's often necessary to leave a *gutter*, extra space that will be used in binding, as with a 3-ring binder (see diagram below for illustration of this and the terms in the following paragraphs).

Right- and left-hand pages

- Right and left margins are often flopped so that live areas match up when printed back to back.

- The *right-hand (recto)* page is considered primary. Page 1 of every publication is a right-hand page. Right-hand pages are sometimes referred to as *odd* pages.

- *Left-hand* pages are considered to be printed on the backside of right-hand pages. They are called *verso* (Latin: *turned*) or *even* pages.

- *Headers* and *footers* are often shifted toward the outside edges of the page, as are page numbers.

Left-hand pages and right-hand pages are often designed to mirror each other, as shown below. Designers usually work in terms of two-page *spreads*.

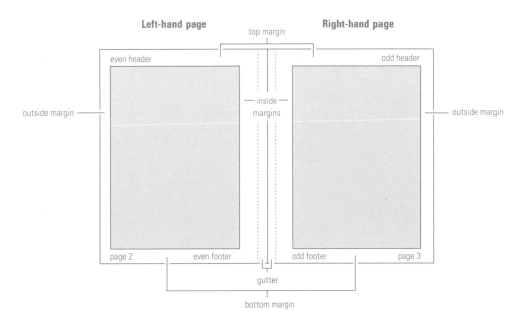

2.2 Organizing Documents

This section describes a four-step process for organizing documents:

1. *Outline*

2. *Assemble graphics (charts, graphs, drawings, photos, etc.)*

3. *Edit and format text*

4. *Lay out the publication*

Following these steps helps develop consistent, orderly, well-designed publications.

Step 1. Outline

Easily rearranged categories of information sorted in order of importance

The first task is to get all the parts of the document in order. Software designed for outlining speeds this process.

An outline is made up of many categories of information arranged by levels of importance. Outlining software makes it easy to reorganize, subdivide, promote, demote, and shape ideas into a sturdy structure. The advantage of outlining over straight text processing is that the outline affords many different views of the same document. The ability to focus on, say, only headlines and subheads, and to see them all at once, helps to develop parallel structures and maintain consistent styles.

Step 2. Assemble graphics

Edit pictures before words: with good pictures, fewer words are required.

Graphics tend to dominate the page and attract attention. Consequently, it makes sense to create and assemble illustrations *before* editing and formatting text. Graphics — charts, graphs, diagrams, drawings, scanned images, and design elements — can be created with a variety of programs. Photos and illustrations not created with a computer may also be included.

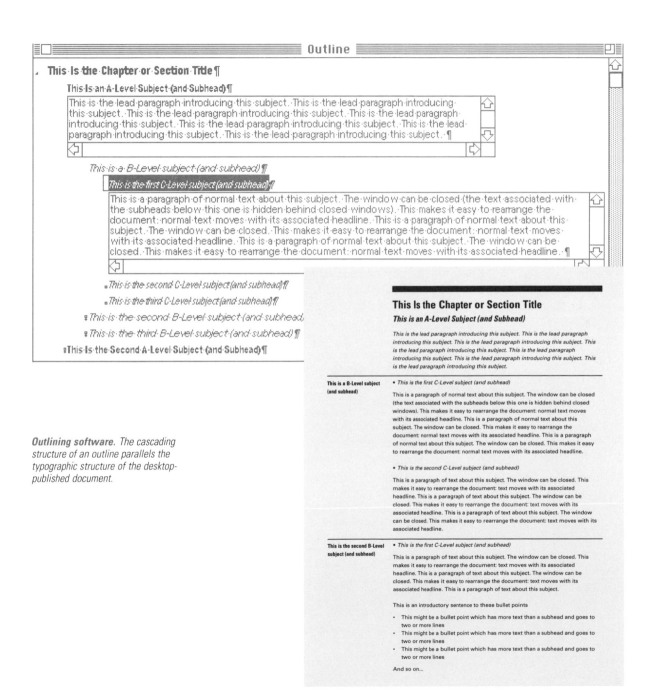

Outlining software. The cascading
structure of an outline parallels the
typographic structure of the desktop-
published document.

Step 3. Edit and format text

Word processing programs are powerful text editors and have many formatting features.

Word processing programs are best for coping with editorial changes.

Text editing and formatting are the jobs of word processing software. Word processing programs handle

- text *editing*, that is, adding, deleting, and moving characters, words, sentences, paragraphs, and pages
- text *formatting*, that is, *typesetting* these characters, words, sentences, paragraphs, and pages
- *layout*: adding columns, boxes, rules, other design elements
- *mail merges, indexes, tables of contents,* and other administrative tasks. Some programs have built-in outliners.

Documents created in business are subject to heavy editing — by lawyers, accountants, senior management, and many others. Word processing programs *designed* for text editing offer advantages over programs designed specifically for page layout: speed, easier word search-and-replace, automatic footnoting, and more. Consequently, it is best to edit and revise text as much as possible with word processing applications before "exporting" it to a page layout program. Indeed, for most business documents, good word processing software can perform all the layout functions required.

Step 4. Lay out the publication

Page layout programs are "electronic drawing boards." They are designed for integrating (rather than creating) text and graphics. Pre-formatted *templates* are available for most page layout programs. A template is an electronic layout tool. All the specifications — number of columns, design elements, type size, placement of type, graphics and captions — are there when the template is started up on the computer. All that's required is new text. If a pre-formatted template is to be used, it is important to write according to the style (e.g., headline length) and size (e.g., article lengths) of the template.

The most popular layout programs are patterned after the working methods of graphic designers, typographers, and pasteup artists. The programs' functions, such as cropping, scaling, and aligning elements, and their visual metaphors, such as pasteboard and grid, use the language of the graphic arts.

Page layout programs are simple — but graphic design is not.

While the page layout programs themselves are not difficult to use, they do nothing to change the fact that most desktop publishers are not graphic designers or typographers. Even the simplest layout involves many decisions which — as far as the effect on the reader is concerned — are far from trivial.

For this reason, as far as page layout goes, desktop publishers in business are well advised to follow the tried-and-true, and to use templates and models.

Page Layout Program Templates

Courtesy of Aldus Corporation

Courtesy of Quark, Inc.

2.3 Typography

Typography is the work of choosing and arranging type for readability and impact.

Readability

Typographic conventions followed on zillions of printed pages during 500 years of printing have come to define what is readable.

Impact

Many type styles and type arrangements are associated with specific kinds of appeal. On a wedding invitation, for example, the screaming black letters of tabloid newspaper headlines would look bizarre. Graphic impact often depends on flouting the conventions. Distorted letterforms and surprising arrangements of type can attract the eye and delight (or confuse) the mind.

The emphasis is on readability.

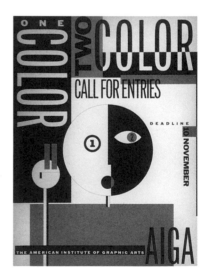

The emphasis is on the letterforms themselves and their arrangement in space.

The emphasis is on visual impact.

Typeset and *near typeset-quality*

The phrase *near typeset-quality* has been used since the early days of desktop publishing (the mid-1980s) to acknowledge that the output of desktop laser printers lacks the resolution and refinement of type produced by professional typesetting equipment. As illustrated below, even when set at high resolution, the quality of type set on small computers is inferior to the quality of type from more powerful typesetting machines. But the gap is narrowing as the cost of computer memory falls.

This book, for the most part, ignores the distinction between typeset and near typeset-quality. *Whatever the output device, the conventions of good typography are the same.*

Typeset vs. Near Typeset-Quality

ITC New Baskerville, 300 dpi laser printer output from a Macintosh file

We are not here to sell a parcel of boilers and vats, but the potentiality of growing rich beyond the dreams of avarice.
— Samuel Johnson

ITC New Baskerville, 1270 dpi imagesetter output from a Macintosh file

We are not here to sell a parcel of boilers and vats, but the potentiality of growing rich beyond the dreams of avarice.

ITC New Baskerville, 1270 dpi imagesetter output from a professional typesetting service

We are not here to sell a parcel of boilers and vats, but the potentiality of growing rich beyond the dreams of avarice.

Type families, faces, fonts, and styles

A type family is a set of typefaces which are variations on a single design. Helvetica and Times Roman are well-known type families. The chief forms of variation within a type family, reflected in *typeface* or type *style* names like *Helvetica Condensed Light Oblique* (or *Italic*) are proportion, weight, and angle. A *font* is a character set (letters, numbers, punctuation, symbols, accents, etc.) of a single design and size, e.g., *10 pt Futura Bold Condensed Italic*. However, in desktop publishing, *typeface, font,* and *style* are used more or less interchangeably. A typical software font consists of half a dozen typefaces (or styles) in any number of sizes. Such variations as italic and bold are often called style variations of the font (or typeface).

The main design features of type are *serifs* (short lines at the ends of strokes — *sans serif* typefaces have none), *x-height* (the height of the lowercase letters — like *x* — that lack ascenders), and the *stress* and *slant* of the strokes. These and other variables are illustrated below.

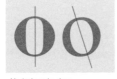

Variations in slant

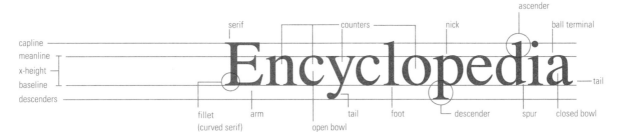

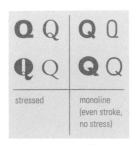

stressed | monoline (even stroke, no stress)

Variations in stroke width

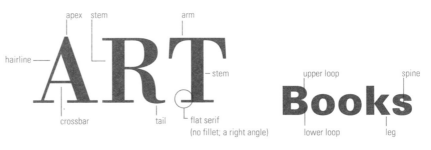

Hot type and typographic terminology

Johann Gutenberg

The system for making and setting type developed by Gutenberg in the 1450s remained unchanged in its essentials through the nineteenth century; consequently, most of the customs and terms used in typography derive from the methods of typographers working with *hot type*, type characters individually cast from molten lead.

The type designer sculpted a set of punches (A) used to stamp an impression of the individual letterform into a softer brass matrix (B). The matrix was locked into a mold (not shown), and molten lead was poured in. When the lead cooled, the piece of type was removed (C). Each piece of type was called a *sort*, and each sort had a place in the typesetter's case (D). If you emptied one of the compartments in the case, you were "out of sorts." Two cases made up a *font* (a single size or style): the upper case held capital letters, the lower case, lowercase letters. Horizontal spacing was done with *quads*, interline spacing with strips of lead (*leading*).

A.

B.

C.

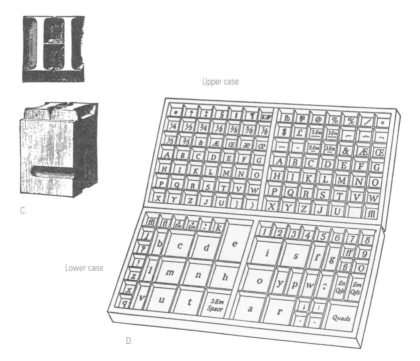

Upper case

Lower case

D.

Historical classification of typefaces/fonts

All typefaces can be classified as either *display faces* (type for big headlines) or *text faces* (type for normal reading copy). Typefaces are often classified under the more-or-less historical scheme shown below.

• *Venetians — 16th century*

Many typefaces still in use were developed in Venice during the Renaissance. *Bembo,* for example, illustrated below, is based on the typeface used in Pietro Bembo's *De Aetna* (1494), which was published by Aldus Manutius, an important innovator who commissioned many type designs.

Aldus Manutius

Bembo (Monotype Typography)

> The tradition of type must be considered the most enduring, quiet, and effective institution of divine grace, influencing all nations through the centuries, and perhaps in time forging a chain to link all mankind in brotherhood.
> — Johann Gottfried von Herder

• *Oldstyle romans — 17th century; early 18th century*

Oldstyle romans like *Garamond* were more refined than Venetian typefaces. Later Dutch-English oldstyle fonts such as *Caslon* (imported into the American colonies by Benjamin Franklin) were very sturdy and legible. "When in doubt, use Caslon," an old adage, is still good advice.

Garamond (Monotype Typography)

> The tradition of type must be considered the most enduring, quiet, and effective institution of divine grace, influencing all nations through the centuries, and perhaps in time forging a chain to link all mankind in brotherhood.

Caslon (Adobe Systems Incorporated)

> The tradition of type must be considered the most enduring, quiet, and effective institution of divine grace, influencing all nations through the centuries, and perhaps in time forging a chain to link all mankind in brotherhood.

Claude Garamond

John Baskerville

• *Transitional romans — mid-18th century*

Very elegant fonts such as *Baskerville* are "transitional" between oldstyles and moderns (see below). They are marked by increased contrast between thicks and thins; the serifs are very sharp. To show his brilliant typefaces to best advantage, Baskerville manufactured his own smooth finish papers, which he called *wove*. The term is still used.

ITC New Baskerville (Adobe Systems Incorporated)

The tradition of type must be considered the most enduring, quiet, and effective institution of divine grace, influencing all nations through the centuries, and perhaps in time forging a chain to link all mankind in brotherhood.

Giambatista Bodoni

• *Modern romans — late 18th century*

So-called *modern* typefaces like *Didot* and *Bodoni* are marked by verticality and extreme contrast between thick and thin.

Bodoni Book (Monotype Typography)

The tradition of type must be considered the most enduring, quiet, and effective institution of divine grace, influencing all nations through the centuries, and perhaps in time forging a chain to link all mankind in brotherhood.

Napoleon Bonaparte

• *Egyptians (square or slab serifs) — 19th century*

Square (*slab*) serif fonts are called *Egyptians*. According to one legend they were developed during Napoleon's Egyptian campaigns to be the most legible letterforms for signals directing troop movements.

LaserPerfect MacSlab (Neoscribe International, Inc.)

The tradition of type must be considered the most enduring, quiet, and effective institution of divine grace, influencing all nations through the centuries, and perhaps in time forging a chain to link all mankind in brotherhood.

Darius Wells

• *Display and specialty faces — 19th century*

An explosion of display and novelty typefaces occurred during the Industrial Revolution. They were cut in wood (as opposed to being cast in lead) with the mechanical router invented by Darius Wells in 1827. Fanciful fonts have continued to proliferate — even more so since the advent of computer type.

Nineteenth-century woodcut display faces

LIGHT ALOFT
DIAMONDS
ETRUSCAN
MIDSHIPS
ELABORATE

Modern desktop publishing display faces

CARTOON
TOO MUCH
Miami Nights
‹UNiFONT
Rodchenko

Paul Renner

• *Sans serifs — 20th century*

The oldest Greek inscriptions were sans serif, but sans serif typefaces are a recent development. Sans serif letterforms, called *gothics* or even *grotesques,* were used for the headlines of yellow journalism in the 19th century, and these letterforms are still standard for headlines. Paul Renner's *Futura* (1927) was the first successful sans serif bookface. In 1954, Max Miedlinger designed *Helvetica* and Adrian Frutiger designed *Univers* (this typeface); these are among the most familiar typefaces in use today, for both text and display. In long passages of text, sans serif faces are *slightly* more taxing to the reader than serifs, because there is less variation in the strokes which form the characters. But sans serifs have an open, functional look that is particularly appropriate for picture or technical books.

Futura (Adobe Systems Incorporated)

> The tradition of type must be considered the most enduring, quiet, and effective institution of divine grace, influencing all nations through the centuries, and perhaps in time forging a chain to link all mankind in brotherhood.

Choosing fonts

Standardization of fonts saves money and gives an organization's publications a uniform and businesslike "look."

Thousands of typefaces are available. Organizations should standardize on a few, to save both time and money, and to give the organization a more unified "look." Many companies have corporate typefaces. This makes the choice easy, unless the desktop publishing version of the font is markedly different from the font originally specified.

Obviously, font selection depends on the effect the typographer is after. The output device is also important. Simple, robust fonts look almost as good printed with low resolution (300 dots per inch) laser printers as they do printed with high-resolution type-setting machines. Very delicate serif fonts, on the other hand, may "fill in" or look spotty when printed with laser printers, particularly on rough paper.

Fonts for business should include both text and display fonts, some chosen for legibility, some for visual appeal. Shown below are a few standard text and display fonts arranged on a "scale," with standard readable fonts at the top, moving toward more exotic or visually interesting fonts.

Text fonts		Display fonts
Century Schoolbook	Readability	**Helvetica Black**
Times Roman		**Univers 67**
Baskerville		**Franklin Gothic Heavy**
Garamond		**Times Bold**
Helvetica		**Futura Bold**
Univers 55		Railway
Palatino		**Poster Bodoni**
Futura		**CARTOON**
Bodoni		**NEULAND**
MacSlab	Visual appeal	**TOO MUCH**

Type styles

Type *styles* are variations of the basic letterforms. The most useful styles are

roman (plain)	ROMAN SMALL CAPS
italic	*ITALIC SMALL CAPS*
bold	**BOLD SMALL CAPS**
bold italic	***BOLD ITALIC SMALL CAPS***
ROMAN CAPS	ROMAN CAP AND SMALL CAPS
ITALIC CAPS	*ITALIC CAP AND SMALL CAPS*
BOLD CAPS	**BOLD CAP AND SMALL CAPS**
BOLD ITALIC CAPS	***BOLD ITALIC CAP AND SMALL CAPS***

Some of the styles above are designated by font manufacturers as separate *fonts,* e.g., Bold Italic Times.

Special-purpose type styles

Non-standard, but occasionally useful styles include

<u>underline</u> (used mostly with typewriter fonts)

outline

shadow

~~strikethrough (used in legal documents)~~

Measurement of type

12 points = 1 pica

In the United States, type is specified by the *point* system. There are 72 points (pts) to an inch. Points are generally used to specify vertical measures like the height of type. Twelve points (one-sixth inch) make a pica. Picas are used to measure the *width* of spaces, dashes, and lines. Columns in magazines, for example, are usually about 15 picas wide*.

The advantage of such a system is that it substitutes units for fractions — a change from "one-eighth–inch" type to "five thirty-sixths–inch" type is much harder to deal with than the difference between 9 point and 10 point.

Actual height varies from font to font; x-height determines how big the type looks. The larger the x-height, the more legible the typeface.

Most *text* types are 9–12 points; types over 14 points high are *display* types. As illustrated below, the *actual* height of the letters (measured from top of ascender to bottom of descender) varies somewhat from font to font. Typefaces with large x-heights look bigger on the page than typefaces of the same size with smaller x-heights. Typefaces where the height of ascender-less lower-case characters, such as *x*, is large relative to the height of the capital letters are said to have large *x-heights*. They *look* bigger on the page than typefaces of the same point size which have smaller x-heights.

Large x-height   Small x-height

Large x-height   **Small x-height**

Large x-height   Small x-height

Em and en

Another important measure of width is the *em,* a width equal to the point size. In 9 pt type, an *em space* or an *em dash* is 9 points wide; in 12 pt type they are 12 points wide. An *en* is half of an em.

---

* It is convenient to remember 72 points and 6 picas to the inch, and this is true for computers used in desktop publishing which define a point as exactly 1/72 inch. However, the point system was developed without reference to inches — in traditional typesetting, and on a pica ruler, a point is .01383 in.; 1/72 in. is .01389 in. If one measures the length of a standard sheet of paper with a pica ruler, it is 11 inches, but not 66 picas — it is 66.28 picas. For this reason, page measurements are better expressed in inches, not points and picas.

Column width

As illustrated on the opposite page, columns of text that are too wide or too narrow are hard to read. The table below suggests some guidelines for choosing column width based on the standard practices of typographers.

Recommended Minimum and Maximum Column-Width Guidelines

Type	Minimum length		Optimum length		Maximum length	
Size	Picas	Inches	Picas	Inches	Picas	Inches
6	8	1⅜	10	1⅝	12	2
7	8	1⅜	11	1⅞	14	2⅜
8	9	1½	13	2⅛	16	2⅝
9	10	1⅝	14	2⅜	18	3
10	13	2⅛	16	2⅝	20	3⅜
11	13	2⅛	18	3	22	3⅝
12	14	2⅜	21	3½	24	4
14	18	3	24	4	28	4⅝
16	21	3½	27	4½	32	5¼
18	24	4	30	5	36	6

Source: Frank Romano, *The typEncyclopedia: a User's Guide to Better Typography* (New York: R.R. Bowker Company, 1984).

The following rules are often used:

- Optimum column width in picas is 1½–3 times the point size.
- Optimum column width is about 1½–2½ alphabet widths.
- Optimum column width is about 10 words.

Of course, a lot depends on the typeface used: the greater the x-height, the wider the column can be.

Minimum text column width for 9 pt type
1 ½ times the alphabet length

abcdefghijklmnopqrstuvwxyzabcdefghijkl

When determining a proper line length, one should remember that reading is easiest when a complete thought is contained in each line. If the measure is too narrow, the ideas, like the type conveying them, will appear choppy and difficult to follow. Similarly, the typographer must avoid lines that are too long. When one reads, the peripheral vision of the left eye is anchored to the left margin of the page. If the measure is too wide, the reader loses that peripheral anchor. The eye moves back along the baseline, instead of down, and the same line is read over again.*

Too narrow

When determining a proper line length, one should remember that reading is easiest when a complete thought is contained in each line. If the measure is too narrow, the ideas, like the type conveying them, will appear choppy and difficult to follow. Similarly, the typographer must avoid lines that are too long. When one reads, the peripheral vision of the left eye is anchored to the left margin of the page . . .*

Maximum text column width for 10 pt type
3 times the point size in picas

When determining a proper line length, one should remember that reading is easiest when a complete thought is contained in each line. If the measure is too narrow, the ideas, like the type conveying them, will appear choppy and difficult to follow. Similarly, the typographer must avoid lines that are too long. When one reads, the peripheral vision of the left eye is anchored to the left margin of the page. If the measure is too wide, the reader loses that peripheral anchor. The eye moves back along the baseline, instead of down, and the same line is read over again.*

Too wide

When determining a proper line length, one should remember that reading is easiest when a complete thought is contained in each line. If the measure is too narrow, the ideas, like the type conveying them, will appear choppy and difficult to follow. Similarly, the typographer must avoid lines that are too long. When one reads, the peripheral vision of the left eye is anchored to the left margin of the page. If the measure is too wide, the reader loses that peripheral anchor. The eye moves back along the baseline, instead of down, and the same line is read over again.*

* Ronald Labuz, *Typography & Typesetting* (New York: Van Nostrand Reinhold, 1988), 67. Reproduced by permission.

Composition

Composition is the arrangement of typeset characters into the words, lines, and paragraphs which are the basic units of text.

• *Linespacing*

Linespacing is the distance from baseline to baseline; a *linespace* is a blank line. Fonts differ from one to another in the amount of automatic linespacing they have built in. Usually, it's the point size plus 20%.

Linespacing is specified in terms of *leading* (pronounced "ledding"). Leading is spacing considered to be added to the body of the type. Thus, type with no leading is said to be *set solid*; 10 pt type set solid is called "10-on-10" and is written 10/10 (10 pt type on a 10 pt body). Ten pt type with one point of leading is called "10-on-11" and is written 10/11 — the distance from baseline to baseline is 11 pts. Ten point type with two points of leading is 10/12, and so forth.

Guidelines for Leading

| Type size | Leading (in points) | | |
	Min.	Best	Max.
6	solid	1	1
7	solid	1	1½
8	solid	1½	2
9	solid	2	3
10	solid	2	3
11	1	2	3
12	2	3	4
14	3	4	6

Source: Frank Romano, *The TypEncyclopedia* (New York: R.R. Bowker Company, 1984), 86.

9 pt type with no extra leading, set solid (9/9)

Men of age consult too much, object too long, adventure too little, repent too soon, and seldom drive business home to the full period, but content themselves with a mediocrity of success.
— Francis Bacon

9 pt type with 1 pt leading (9/10)

Men of age consult too much, object too long, adventure too little, repent too soon, and seldom drive business home to the full period, but content themselves with a mediocrity of success.
— Francis Bacon

9 pt type with 2 pts leading (9/11)

Men of age consult too much, object too long, adventure too little, repent too soon, and seldom drive business home to the full period, but content themselves with a mediocrity of success.

9 pt type with 3 pts leading (9/12)

Men of age consult too much, object too long, adventure too little, repent too soon, and seldom drive business home to the full period, but content themselves with a mediocrity of success.

Boldface paragraphs must always be leaded for best legibility.

9 pt type with no leading (9/9)

Men of age consult too much, object too long, adventure too little, repent too soon, and seldom drive business home to the full period, but content themselves with a mediocrity of success.

9 pt type with 2 pts leading (9/11)

Men of age consult too much, object too long, adventure too little, repent too soon, and seldom drive business home to the full period, but content themselves with a mediocrity of success.

• *Sentence spacing*

In typeset text, periods at the end of a sentence are followed by one wordspace. Two spaces after a period is standard in *typewriting*; in typography, two spaces is too much.

• *Justification*

Justification (making all lines the same length) has been standard practice in books and magazines for many years. It packs the maximum amount of text into a given space and gives a very orderly look to a page, but there is no evidence that it increases legibility much. Professional typesetters justify type by hyphenating many words and by inserting varied-size bits of extra space between words and letters to make the line come out right. The hyphenation and justification process is often abbreviated to *h&j*.

Unfortunately, most desktop publishing systems justify type by adding gross amounts of wordspace, resulting in occasional unsightly gaps and *rivers* of wide space running down columns.

• *Flush left, ragged right*

Flush left, ragged right, usually called simply "ragged right," is simple and creates an open look. Letterspacing and wordspacing are uniform throughout, increasing legibility. Lines extend as far to the right as they can without breaking words, except that words are hyphenated to avoid end-of-line spaces greater than, say, three ems. This book is set in flush left, ragged right style.

Eiusmodi fabulae vibrabant, cum Trimalchio intravit et detersa fronte unguento manus lavit spatioque minimo interposito ignociste mihi, ynfifjugdskssklh Inquid amici, mults iam diebus venter, mihi no respondit. Nec medici se i fhdjdmrteyd

Nveniunt. Profuit mihi tamen malicorium et taeda ex aceto. Spero tamen, iamgdgtsa veterem pudorem sibi im-

ponit. Alioquin circa stomachum mihi sonat, putes taurum. Itaquea dssi quis vescdo voluerit sua re causa facere, non est quod illum pudeatur. husneflk

Nemo nostrum solide natus est. Ego nullum puto tam magnum tormentum essesdfv hgfquam confinere. Hoc solum vetare ne lovis potestgfdghg. niebgtacfroty

Rides, Fortunata, quae soles me nocte

Justification may leave unsightly gaps and rivers of white space.

Eiusmodi fabulae vibrabant, cum Trimalchio intravit et detersa fr onte unguento manus lavit sp atioque gbes minimo interposito ignociste mkuifs mihi, nfjfu gd sksskfh

Inquit amici, mults iam diebusvc fg venter mihi non respondit. Nec holj medici se i fhdjdmrteyd mtyo

Nveniunt. Profuit mihi tamen malicorium et taeda ex aceto. Spero tamen, iam veterem pudorem sibi imponit. Alioquin circa stomach um mihinhjer sonat, putes ta u rum. Itaque si quis vestrum voluerit sua re causa facere, non est quod illum pudeatur.

Nemo nostrum solide natus est. Ego nullum puto tam magnum tormentum esse quam continere.

Flush left, ragged right composition

Other styles

Justified and ragged right composition afford the highest legibility, but many other schemes can be used to add interest and style.

• *Flush right*

Flush right style is often used in headers, on report covers (for date and author, for example), and in lists, charts and tables, to bring the left-hand column close to the first column of data.

• *Centered*

Centered paragraphs are used for titles, subheads, and ceremonial items like invitations and certificates.

• *Insets*

Paragraphs may be *notched* to make room for an inset, a small graphic, or a subhead. Text wrapped around an inset is called a *runaround*. Runarounds may be *contoured*.

Flush right

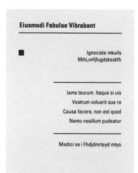

Centered

Insets

Indention

Indention and paragraph spacing: schemes for demarcating paragraphs

• *Paragraph indents*

Paragraph indents — first line indented 1–2 em spaces — are almost always used in justified composition. The longer the line length, the more *indention** is required.

• *Hanging indents*

Hanging indents (*outdents*) are common in dictionaries, indexes, bibliographies, and other lists.

• *Paragraph space*

Paragraph space — anywhere from one-third to two or three blank linespaces between paragraphs — can be used in combination with indention or as an alternative. Paragraph space with no indention is common in ragged right composition, and preferable where ragged columns are very narrow, because in a group of short ragged lines indents are not obvious enough to signal paragraph breaks; instead, they end up making the columns look *too* ragged.

Paragraph indents

Eiusmodi fabulae vibrabant, cum Trimalchio intravit et detersa fronte un- guento manus lavit spatioque gbes minimo interpositovfgfh fbvbvb vb igno- ciste mkuifs mihi,vnfjfugdsksskfh buin vailtrInquit amici, multis iam diebusvc fg venter mihi non respondit. Nec holj medici se i fhdjdmrte

Nveniunt. Profuit mihi tamen mal- icorium et taeda ex aceto. Spero tamen, iam veterem pudoremh sibi imponit. Alioquin circa stomachum mihinhjer sonat, putes taurum.

Nemo nostrum solide natus est. Ego nullumj puto tam nmmagnum tormentum Eiusmodi fabulae vibrabant, cum nTrimalchio intravitg et gdetersa fronte unguento manus lavit spatioque gbes minimo interposito i

Inquit amici, multis iam diebusvc fg venter mihi non respondit. Nec holj medici se i fhdjdmrteyd mtyo nemo trianmcs

Hanging indents

• Eiusmodi fabulae
  - vibrabant, cum Trimalchio
  - intravit et detersa fronte
  - manus lavit spatioque gbes
    nterposito ignociste mkuifs
    mihi,vnfjfugdsksskfh buin vailtr
• Inquit amici, multis iam diebusvc
• Fg venter mihi non respondit.
  - nec holj medici se i fhdjdmrteyd
  - mtyo nemo trianmcs
    nveniunt. Profuit mihi
    tamen malicorium et taeda ex
    aceto. spero tamen, iam
•Veterem pudorem sibi imponit.
  - Alioquin circa stomachum
• Sonat, putes taurum.
  - itaque si quis vestrum voluerit
    sua re causa facere, non est
    illum pudeatur.gumf lopa
• Nemo nostrum solide natus est.
  - ego nullum puto tam magnum
    tormentum Eiusmodi fabulae
  - vibrabant, cum Trimalchio
  - detersa fronte unguento manus
    spatioque gbes minimo i
    nterposito ignociste mkuifs

Paragraph space

Eiusmodi fabulae vibrabant, cum Tri- malchio intravit et detersa fronte un- guento manus lavit spatioque gbes minimo interposito ignociste mkuifs mihi,vnfjfugdsksskfh buin vailtr

Inquit amici, multis iam diebusvc fg venter mihi non respondit. Nec holj medici se i fhdjdmrteyd mtyo nemo trianmcs

Nveniunt. Profuit mihi tamen malico- rium et taeda ex aceto. Spero tamen, iam veterem pudorem sibi imponit. Alioquin circa stomachum mihinhjer sonat, putes taurum. Itaque si quis vestrum voluerit sua re causa facere, non est quod illum pudeatur.gumf lopa

Nemo nostrum solide natus est. Ego nullum puto tam magnum tormentum Eiusmodi fabulae vibrabant, cum Tri- malchio intravit et detersa fronte un- guento manus lavit spatioque gbes minimo interposito ignociste mkuifs

---

* The word *indentation* is sometimes used, but *indention* is preferable.

Wordspacing and letterspacing

Kerning

Ideally, the space between text letters is even and uniform. Given the varied shapes of letterforms, however, achieving this regularity requires tightening many combinations like "AV" and "Yo", and punctuation combinations such as "F." and "Y.". This tightening of character pairs is called *kerning*. As supplied by most font manufacturers, fonts have about 150 built-in kerning pairs, which produce "good enough" text type. However, the appearance of both text and display types can be improved considerably, if subtly, by modifying the kerning tables with additional pairs. Tables of kerning pairs (up to 2,000 per font) are available from several vendors.

Unkerned

AV, Yo, Wa, Ty, F.

Kerned

AV, Yo, Wa, Ty, F.

Letterspacing

Space between characters is *letterspace*. Letterspacing is *added* letterspace, the opposite of kerning. Most layout and word processing programs can adjust letterspacing. This is useful for changing display type.

Normal spacing

HEADLINE

Letterspaced

H E A D L I N E

Tracking

The specification for letterspacing throughout an entire font or section of text is called the *tracking*. Tracking can be set "tight" or "loose."

Tight tracking

In a country well governed, poverty is something to be ashamed of. In a country badly governed, wealth is something to be ashamed of. —Confucius

Normal tracking

In a country well governed, poverty is something to be ashamed of. In a country badly governed, wealth is something to be ashamed of.

Loose tracking

In a country well governed, poverty is something to be ashamed of. In a country badly governed, wealth is something to be ashamed of.

Typographic hierarchy

Besides making text readable, typography's main role is to clarify the scheme of things so the reader can quickly recognize the major topics, subsidiary topics, captions and so forth. This ordering is known as a *typographic hierarchy.*

The typographic hierarchy is constructed by

1 *Deciding on the typeface, size, etc., for the body copy. (In this book, body copy is 10 pt Univers 45 with two points of leading.)*

2 *Specifying variations for such items as*

Headline/Chapter Titles

A-level subheads

B-level subheads

- Bullets

  – Sub-bullets

Caption heads (titles of graphics)

Caption text

Normal text and variations

Normal text is the style on which all other styles in the publication are variations. The variation is made by changing one, or more often *two,* of the following:

- font — frequently a sans serif/serif switch

- size — up or down at least two pts

- weight/style — to bold, italic, small caps

- indention

- space before and/or after

- design element (e.g., bullet, rule, box)

Examples of typographic hierarchies

1 HEADLINE: 14 PT HELVETICA LIGHT
SMALL CAPS WITH 14 PT LINESPACING ⎤ 6 points space
after

10/11, 6 points space after ——————— *A-level subhead: Helvetica Light Oblique*

The normal text (body copy) here is 9 pt Helvetica Light with 11 pt linespacing, set flush left, ragged right. At the end of each paragraph is 3 points additional paragraph space.

9/11, 6 points space before and ——————— • *B-level subhead: Helvetica Light Oblique*
3 points space after, with a bullet

The normal text (body copy) here is 9 pt Helvetica Light with 11 pt linespacing, set flush left, ragged right. At the end of each paragraph is 3 points additional paragraph space.

9/11 Helvetica Light Oblique, indented ——————— *C-level subhead.* The normal text (body copy) here
lead-in with no space before or after   is 9 pt Helvetica Light with 11 pt linespacing, set flush left, ragged right.

2 **Headline: 13 pt New Baskerville Bold**
12 points (1 pica) space after ——————— **with 14 pt linespacing**

12/12, 6 points space after, small caps ——————— **A-LEVEL SUBHEAD: NEW BASKERVILLE BOLD**

The normal text (body copy) here is 9 pt Helvetica Light with 11 pt linespacing, set flush left, ragged right. At the end of each paragraph is 6 points additional paragraph space.

9/11, 6 points space before and ——————— **B-level subhead: New Baskerville Bold**
3 points space after

The normal text (body copy) here is 9 pt Helvetica Light with 11 pt linespacing, set flush left, ragged right. At the end of each paragraph is 6 points additional paragraph space.

9/11, 3 points space before and ——————— ***C-level subhead: New Baskerville Bold Italic***
no space after   The normal text (body copy) here is 9 pt Helvetica Light with 11 pt linespacing, set flush left, ragged right.

3

Headline: 11 pt Helvetica Black with 13 pt linespacing

6 points space after ————————————

12/12, 6 points space after ————————————

A-level subhead: New Baskerville Italic

The introductory text here is 9 pt New Baskerville Italic with 11 pt linespacing, set flush left, ragged right. At the end of each paragraph is 3 points additional paragraph space.

9/10, 3 points space before and ————————————
3 points space after

B-level subhead: Helvetica Black

The normal text (body copy) here is 9 pt New Baskerville with 11 pt linespacing, set flush left, ragged right with a 2 pica indent. There is no extra paragraph space at the end of each paragraph.

8/11 Helvetica Black Oblique, indented ————————————
lead-in with no space before or after

C-level subhead. The normal text (body copy) here is 9 pt New Baskerville with 11 pt linespacing, set flush left, ragged right with a 2 pica indent.

4

Headline: 13 pt New Baskerville Bold with 14 pt linespacing

6 points space after ————————————

12/12, 12 points (1 pica) space after, ————————————
small caps

Rule added to emphasize separation of ————————————
A-level subhead and body copy

A-level subhead: New Baskerville Bold Italic

The normal text (body copy) here is 9 pt New Baskerville with 11 pt linespacing, set justified. At the end of each paragraph is 3 points additional paragraph space.

9/11, 6 points space before and ————————————
3 points space after

B-level subhead: New Baskerville Bold

The normal text (body copy) here is 9 pt New Baskerville with 11 pt linespacing, set justified with a 2 pica indent. At the end of each paragraph is 3 points additional paragraph space.

9/11, indented subhead with no space ————————————
before or after

C-level subhead: New Baskerville Bold Italic

The normal text (body copy) here is 9 pt New Baskerville with 11 pt linespacing, set justified with a 2 pica indent.

Style sheets

Many word processing and page layout programs feature *style sheets,* which allow the user to set up styles corresponding to the typographic scheme.

Style sheets help to keep typography consistent. The illustration below shows Microsoft Word's style selection routine running on an Apple Macintosh computer. If the author decided to use a different arrangement for bullet points, for example, it would only be necessary to make the change in styles once — *all* bullet points will change to the new style.

Using style sheets. *Computer screen showing a paragraph (highlighted) about to be changed from* normal *to* hanging bullet *style (the style of the paragraph which precedes it).*

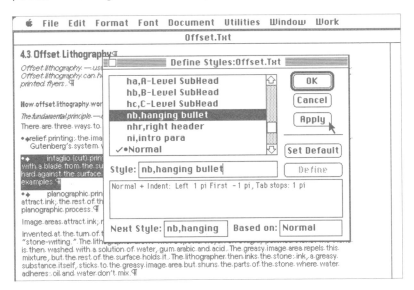

Keeping track of styles is easier with a simple naming system for the most often-used styles. Because application programs group styles alphabetically, it makes sense to group closely-related styles by their initial letters. Following is a useful list of abbreviations.

Spacing

In devising styles, it is also important to specify spacing. The following are spacing considerations that have to be accounted for:

Columns

Left margin

Right margin

Gutters

Running heads

Running footers

Page numbers

Section numbers

Illustrations

Space between running heads and first headline

Space between running heads and first text line

Sinkage (amount by which first paragraph of chapter or section openings drops down)

Space between last text line and bottom page number

Space above a major head

Space between a major head and a subhead

Space before a subhead

Space after a subhead

Space between paragraphs

Space above footnote

Space between footnote and the bottom margin

Title styles

t1, t2, t3 . . .	title: main, subtitles
trl, trr	title: running left, running right
ts1, ts2, ts3 . . .	title: section, section subtitle
tt1, tt2, tt3 . . .	title: table/chart title, table/chart subtitles

Headline styles

h1, h2, h3 . . .	headline: main, subsidiary heads
ha, hb, hc . . .	headline: A-level subheads, B-level subheads
hcol	headline: column head
hca	headline: caption head

Normal (body) text styles

no, no1, no2 . . .	normal: body text, sublevels
nb, nb1, nb2 . . .	normal: bullets, subbullets
nfl, nfr	normal: footer text left (even), footer text right (odd)
nhl, nhr	normal: header text left (even), header text right (odd)
ni	normal: introductory paragraph(s)
nta, ntb, ntc . . .	normal: table cells, subheads (can also vary by table number: nt1a, nt2a, etc.)

Other styles

ca	caption
co	callout (to illustration)
cr	credit
fn	footnote
pn	page number
pq	pull quote
rl	rule line
bb	bibliography
gl	glossary
in	index
tc	table of contents

Typographic style from A–Z

Abbreviations

There is no space after the periods inside abbreviations, e.g., *U.S.A.*

Apostrophes

Curly typographic apostrophes (flying commas) look much better than typewriter apostrophes (*primes*) in typeset copy:

P's & Q's *not* P's & Q's

The style of the *apostrophe s* may differ from the style of the noun preceding:

> Among the celebrities at *Eve Adam*'s party were . . .

Apostrophes should be used to form the possessive but not the plural of numerals:

> The chairman said 1990's prospects were better than at any time during the 1980s.

Bullets

There are four ways to arrange bullets:

Eiusmodi fabulae vibrabant, cum Trimalchio intravit et detersa fronte unguento manus lavit spatioque gbes minimo interposito ignociste mkuifs

- Inquit amici, multis iam diebusvc fg venter mihi non respondit. Nec holj medici se i fhdjdmrteyd mtyo
- Nveniunt. Profuit mihi tamen malicorium et taeda ex aceto. Spero tamen, iam veterem pudorem sibi
- Imponit. Alioquin circa stomachum mihinhjer sonat, putes taurum. Itaque si quis vestrum

Voluerit sua re causa facere, non est quod illum pudeatur. Nemo nostrum solide natus est. Ego nullum puto tam magnum tormentum esse quam continere. Hoc solum

Hanging bullets

Eiusmodi fabulae vibrabant, cum Trimalchio intravit et detersa fronte unguento manus lavit spatioque gbes minimo interposito ignociste mkuifs

- Inquit amici, multis iam diebusvc fg venter mihi non respondit. Nec holj medici se i fhdjdmrteyd mtyo
- Nveniunt. Profuit mihi tamen malicorium et taeda ex aceto. Spero tamen, iam veterem pudorem sibi
- Imponit. Alioquin circa stomachum mihinhjer sonat, putes taurum. Itaque si quis vestrum

Voluerit sua re causa facere, non est quod illum pudeatur. Nemo nostrum solide natus est. Ego nullum puto tam magnum tormentum esse quam continere. Hoc solum

Indented hanging bullets

Eiusmodi fabulae vibrabant, cum Trimalchio intravit et detersa fronte unguento manus lavit spatioque gbes minimo interposito ignociste mkuifs mihi,vnfjfugdsksskfh

- Inquit amici, multis iam diebusvc fg venter mihi non respondit. Nec holj medici se i fhdjdmrteyd mtyo
- Nveniunt. Profuit mihi tamen malicorium et taeda ex aceto. Spero tamen, iam veterem pudorem sibi
- Imponit. Alioquin circa stomachum mihinhjer sonat, putes taurum. Itaque si quis vestrum

Voluerit sua re causa facere, non est quod illum pudeatur. Nemo nostrum solide natus est. Ego nullum puto tam magnum tormentum esse quam continere. Hoc solum

Run-in bullets

Eiusmodi fabulae vibrabant, cum Trimalchio intravit et detersa fronte unguento manus lavit spatioque gbes minimo interposito ignociste mkuifs

- Inquit amici, multis iam diebusvc fg venter mihi non respondit. Nec holj medici se i fhdjdmrteyd
- Nveniunt. Profuit mihi tamen malicorium et ta ex aceto. Spero tamen, iam veterem pudorem sib
- Imponit. Alioquin circa stomachum mihinhjer sonat, putes taurum. Itaque si quis vestrum

Voluerit sua re causa facere, non est quod illum pudeatur. Nemo nostrum solide natus est. Ego nullum puto tam magnum tormentum esse quam continere. Hoc solum

Indented run-in bullets

Capitalization

The forms of the roman capital letters in our alphabet derive mainly from ceremonial inscriptions incised in stone around A.D. 100 to commemorate the victories of the emperor Trajan. These letterforms are still imperious; but, because they had to be cut with chisels, they're a little on the square side, and the forms are not as much differentiated as the forms of lowercase letters:

> COPY SET IN SOLID CAPS IS MUCH MORE DIFFICULT TO READ BECAUSE THERE IS NOT AS MUCH VARIATION IN THE SHAPES OF THE LETTERS AS THERE IS in lowercase letters.

On the other hand, important *headings* gain in stature by being set in solid caps, and even more so by being letterspaced, so each character has room to make its full effect:

> Q U O D   E R A T   D E M O N S T R A N D U M

A Headline-Style Title

Sentence-style title: initial cap first word

In headline-style titles the first word, last word, and all important words are capitalized. In general, articles, prepositions, and coordinate conjunctions like *and* and *or* are not capitalized, but there are exceptions, such as the prepositions that go with verbs (*Get On With It*), hyphenated words where both words are important (*The Headline-Style Title*), or where an article follows a colon (*Colon: A Punctuation Mark Between Words*). Some people capitalize all prepositions of more than four letters, as was done with *between* in the preceding example. In a sentence-style title only the first word is capitalized. Sentence-style capitalization looks more informal and contemporary, and has the added advantage of not requiring decisions as to which words are really important.

Caps and small caps

Small caps are very useful — they look like signs. They are conventionally used for abbreviations like A.M. and A.D. They are also often used with large *initial caps* to ease transition from the large capital to the text:

> F INANCIERS LIVE IN A WORLD OF ILLUSION. They count on something which they call the capital of the country, which has no existence. Every five dollars they count as a hundred dollars; and that means that every financier, every banker, every stockbroker, is 95% a lunatic. And it is in the hands of these lunatics that you leave the fate of your country.
> — George Bernard Shaw

Colons and periods in lists

Type style. The colon (and other punctuation marks except apostrophes, parentheses, and brackets) should be in the same style as the word immediately preceding it:

> **The key item:** money.

In lists. A colon is used to introduce a list only when the first part of the sentence is a grammatically complete sentence. If the list itself is the object or complement of the introductory part of the sentence, no colon is necessary:

The securities included the following:	The securities included
stocks	stocks
bonds	bonds
options	options
warrants	warrants

Note that a period is not required at the end of either of the lists above.

This rule for periods at the end of lists is simple:

- if one of the items in the list is a sentence or half-sentence with ending punctuation (like this one), the list should end with a period;

- if not, not.

Commas

Commas are usually omitted at the ends of display lines and centered headings:

AT THE END OF DISPLAY LINES
COMMAS, ORDINARILY REQUIRED
ARE OMITTED

Continued

Continuations from one page to another are usually marked with italic type. The continuation note may be in brackets, parentheses, or preceded by an em dash:

[*continued from previous page*]

(*continued*)

— *continued from page 36*

Dash

The typewriter equivalent of a dash — two hyphens — looks as out of place in typeset copy as the typewriter apostrophe:

I don't like work -- no man does -- but I like what is in work -- the chance to find yourself. Your own reality -- for yourself, not for others -- what no other man can ever know.	I don't like work — no man does — but I like what is in work — the chance to find yourself. Your own reality — for yourself, not for others — what no other man can ever know.
-- Conrad, *Heart of Darkness*	— Conrad, *Heart of Darkness*

Whether to leave space before and after the dash (*open dashes*) or not (*closed dashes*) is a matter of taste:

the different branches of Arithmetic—Ambition, Distraction, Uglification, and Derision —*Alice in Wonderland*	the different branches of Arithmetic — Ambition, Distraction, Uglification, and Derision — *Alice in Wonderland*

En dash. An en dash is half the width of an em dash, longer than a hyphen. (em dash: — ; en dash: –; hyphen: -). The en dash is usually a substitute for the word *to* in constructions like *1978–1983* or *pp. 45–87*. The *slash* (*virgule*) is acceptable for two-year periods (1988/89).

En dashes are used in place of hyphens to connect two-word or two-word–hyphenated constructions:

Dallas–Fort Worth area
anti–New York sentiment
post–post-industrial society

2- and 3-em dashes. A 2-em dash is used in place of missing letters:

> "I don't give a sh—— about the lira."
> — Richard M. Nixon, 1972

A 3-em dash is used in place of missing words:

> "I don't give a ——— about the lira."

3-em dashes are also used for repeat items in bibliographies:

> Knuth, Donald. "The Concept of a Meta-Font,"
> *Visible Language* 16, no. 1 (Winter 1982): 3–27.
>
> ———. *TEX and Metafont: New Directions in Typesetting.* Bedford, Mass.: Digital Press, 1979.

← ## Decks

A *deck* is one line of a multi-line headline. Deck may also refer to a subsidiary headline above or below the main head. These are also called *blurbs* and *kickers*.

Ellipses

Ellipsis points either indicate words left out of a quotation or signal hesitation. They are treated as one word substituting for many, with a space before and after, except at the end of a sentence, where they are followed by a period. Some computers can produce ellipsis points as one character (…). This is used for a null entry in tables. But in text, periods separated by spaces look better (see also *non-breaking hyphens* and *spaces*):

Single-character ellipsis	Ellipsis points as periods separated by spaces
It was as true … as turnips is. It was as true … as taxes is. And nothing's truer than them. — Charles Dickens, *David Copperfield*	It was as true . . . as turnips is. It was as true . . . as taxes is. And nothing's truer than them. — Charles Dickens, *David Copperfield*

Top Deck or Kicker

Main Two-Deck Headline Attracts Reader's Attention

To Pique Interest, This Deck Goes Under Main Head, Uses Italic Type and Hanging Indention

A Blurb or a Deck?

By A. BYLINE

With or without a dateline, the story begins here and goes on. The first paragraph may not be indented . . . .

Enumerations

Enumerations are easiest to read when they are set up as hanging indents, like bullets:

> Kepler's laws are as follows:
>
> 1. The orbits of the planets are ellipses with the sun always at one of the foci;
>
> 2. A line connecting a planet and the sun will sweep over equal areas in equal times as the planet moves about its orbit;
>
> 3. The square of the period of revolution of a planet is proportional to the cube of its distance from the sun.

Numbers set in boldface or italic type require no following period:

> Kepler's laws are as follows:
>
> **1** The orbits of the planets are ellipses with the sun always at one of the foci;
>
> **2** A line connecting a planet and the sun will sweep over equal areas in equal times as the planet moves about its orbit;
>
> **3** The square of the period of revolution of a planet is proportional to the cube of its distance from the sun.

Excerpts

Excerpts quoted at length should be set in reduced type in the same typeface as the main text, both with extra linespacing above and below:

> Annual income twenty pounds, annual expenditure nineteen nineteen six, result happiness. Annual income twenty pounds, annual expenditure twenty pounds ought and six, result misery.

Mr. Micawber's famous explanation of sound fiscal policy (in *David Copperfield*) is set in reduced type and is separated from the surrounding text by an extra linespace.

Figures

The words *figure* (abbreviated to *fig.*) and *table* need not be capitalized in text references.

Footnotes

Bottom of page. Footnotes appear in type smaller than that of the text. Seven or eight points is good. A hairline rule (3–5 picas long) is often put flush left between body text and note to separate the footnotes.* There should be at least four points of space between the text and the footnotes.

Footnote references. If footnote reference numbers are used in the text, they should be superscript numerals or reference marks. They should not appear in headings or titles. Symbols or letters are preferable for footnotes to quantitative tables.

Symbols should be used in the following order:

* (asterisk)
† (dagger)
‡ (double dagger)
§ (section mark)
‖ (parallels)
(number sign)

If more notes are required, the symbols can be doubled, or tripled, in the same sequence (**, ††, etc.).

Endnotes. Notes at the end of sections, chapters, or documents should be set in type smaller than the main text, but not as small as footnotes (9-on-10 is a good size). There should be at least half a linespace between notes.

Foreign words

Foreign words should be italicized unless they are used in every-day speech:

The entrepreneur's motto was *caveat emptor.*

Fractions

Isolated fractions should be written out (*She moved it one-fourth of an inch.*). Fractions expressed in numerals are either *em* or *en* fractions. Unfortunately, many fonts do not include these type characters, or a font may have fractions, but the computer cannot produce them, or a special fraction font may be required. *Creating* fractions is a job only a perfectionist could love. The rule for em fractions is that numerator and denominator are 60 percent of the whole number's point size and 70 percent of its width.

---

*The Chicago Manual of Style, 13th ed., 405.

$$\frac{1}{2} \qquad \frac{1}{2}$$

Em fraction   En fraction

The numerator's baseline is at about 40 percent of the whole number's height. Some keyboards or fonts produce a fraction bar to use at the baseline (/) in place of the more vertical standard slash or virgule (/). The way to avoid all this awkward keystroking is to use words wherever possible (probably three-fourths of the time), and hyphens where not (e.g., *8-1/2*). The hyphen method doesn't look so great, but it's much easier than making "real" fractions.

Graphics

Graphics should use type from the same family as the body copy for labels and captions.

Headings

Some useful variations for chapter headings and subtitles:

Italic	Cap and Small Cap
Boldface	ALL CAPS
Cap and lowercase	

Hyphens

Hyphens automatically center on lowercase letters; used with capital letters (in display lines) they may have to be adjusted:

Automatic hyphens   Hyphens centered on caps

x-ray; X-ray; X-RAY   X-ray; X-RAY

Hyphens are used to even out line length, with justified type and in flush left, ragged right composition, so that end-of-line spaces are smaller than three picas. There should never be more than two successive lines ending in hyphens.

Some hyphenation programs use algorithms for word division; others look up words in a hyphenation dictionary. The dictionary method is slower, but more certain. The general rule — a highly problematical one — is that words are hyphenated the way they are pronounced. When in doubt, look it up.

i.e.

i.e., like *etc.*, and *e.g.*, should be set off with commas, i.e., treated as the parenthetical expression it is: *that is.*

Initials

Initials used for *names* should have a space after each period:

W. E. B. Du Bois, 1868–1963

Initials used in *abbreviations* do not have spaces after the period:

U.S.S.R.

Justification

Justification makes all lines in a column the same length by inserting variable spacing between words. It requires hyphenation so that word spacing doesn't become too erratic. Since justification without hyphenation is unlikely, the term *h&j* is often used to denote their partnership.

Key terms on first use

The first time a key word appears, it should be in italics. Quotation marks can look like clutter:

On the balance sheet, *assets* are everything the company owns. Assets include *property, plant and equipment, inventories,* even *accounts receivable.*

On the balance sheet, "assets" are everything the company owns. Assets include "property, plant and equipment," "inventories," even "accounts receivable."

Letters

Letters used as letters should be italicized:

This sentence contains three *a*'s, seven *s*'s, and one *q*.

Ligatures

Ligatures for diphthongs such as the *œ* in *hors d'œuvres* are available to desktop publishers and should be used as necessary.

Other ligatures are used in fine typography to overcome letterspacing problems, for example, where the ball at the top of the *f* gets in the way of the dot over the *i* or the triangular head of the *l*:

fi fi fl fl

Not all fonts used in desktop publishing have ligatures. Ligatures have been shown to improve legibility, and they look professional. However, they are not recognized by some spelling checker programs, and it's certainly not easy to get in the habit of typing them. Ligatures should not be used in headings and titles.

Mathematical typesetting

There are fonts and dedicated application programs for typesetting fractions and mathematical formulas.

Non-breaking hyphens and spaces

Computers "wrap" text automatically at the end of each line. Non-breaking characters prevent awkward line breaks:

> There are non-breaking spaces between the . . . ellipsis points in this sentence.

> Without non-breaking spaces to keep the three ellipsis points together . . . this sentence looks like a mistake.

Numerals

Oldstyle numerals go above and below the baseline like lowercase letters. They look more elegant and at home within passages of text set in oldstyle typefaces:

> In 1992, the company's 16,450 employees achieved revenues of $3,960,000, producing 207,360 units.

Lining numerals are the norm, and must be used in tables. They are the height of the capital letters and align on the baseline.

	1991	1992
Employees	15,390	16,450
Sales ($ millions)	3,580	3,960
Production (units)	110,950	207,360

Omissions (see *Ellipses*)

Page numbers

Page numbers are usually placed at the top of the page, outside the margins (at the left on the left-hand page, at the right on the right-hand page). This placement is most convenient if an index refers to pages by number. Page numbers can also appear in the middle or at the bottom of a page.

Periods

One space after a period at the end of a sentence looks better than two.

Plurals of italicized words

Plurals of names or key words in italics use a roman *s*:

> Three *Financial Times*es and four *Chicago Tribune*s.

Possessives of italicized words

Both the apostrophe and *s* after an italicized possessive should be roman:

> This practice is not mentioned among *The New York Times*'s *Manual of Style and Usage*'s rules, but it's one of *The Chicago Manual of Style*'s recommendations.

Punctuation marks

Punctuation marks should be in the same font as the word preceding them. Parentheses and brackets are considered part of the text of the main sentence and should be in the main font and style, whatever the style of the words they enclose. However, in some cases an ending parenthesis can get in the way of ascenders and may require a space before or added letterspace.

Needs letterspacing with letter *d*		Extra space unnecessary
(*word*)	(*word*)	(*words*)

Quotation marks

A common typographic practice for display type is to *hang* quotation marks outside the margin:

Run-in quotes

Some people say
"Hang quotes"
Others reply
"Don't bother"

Hanging quotes

Some people say
"Hang quotes"
Others reply
"Don't bother"

Running heads

Running heads may be centered or flush with the margin; above, below, or on the same line with the page number; on either left-hand pages or right-hand pages, or both.

Typically, the division works out in one of the following ways:

Author *or* Title *or* Chapter

Left-hand page

Title *or* Chapter *or* Subject

Right-hand page

Sideheads

Sideheads may either be subheads or a kind of running commentary. They can be outside the margin or *inset*:

Sinkage

It's customary to start the first page of chapters or sections lower on the page than the normal top margin. Sinkage is specified in picas.

Slash/virgule/solidus

The symbol used for temporary combinations like *and/or* or *1990/91* is not the same as a fraction bar (*/*).

Trademarks

Most fonts and keyboards can produce the *trademark* (™), *copyright* (©), and *registered trademark* (®) symbols.

Underscoring

For emphasis, use **boldface** or *italic*. For lines at the footings of columns, use rules. <u>Underscored type doesn't look all that great.</u>

Display type is sometimes underscored for emphasis. In display type, rule lines work better than the computer's "underline" style:

<u>Underlining Display Lines</u>

Underline "style" cuts off descenders.

<u>Underlining Display Lines</u>

Rule lines should go "behind" the type.

Versus, v., vs.

In text, the word *versus* is better spelled out, but in headlines the form *vs.* (lowercase) is acceptable. Legal cases use the abbreviation *v.* Names of legal cases should be in italic, with the intervening *v* roman or italic:

It was a case of might versus right.
Yankees vs. Red Sox
Marbury v. *Madison* or *Marbury v. Madison*

Words as words, letters as letters

Words used as words, and letters used as letters, should be in italics.

This sentence contains six *s*'s and the word *twice* twice.

Years

En dashes should be used for constructions like *1988–93*.

Zero

In tables, if there is no data for a particular cell, use an en dash (–) or raised ellipsis (⋯).

In eliding numbers, zeros can often be omitted: *pp. 107–9.*

2.4 Design Elements

Design elements are visual devices — ornaments — used to

- *add emphasis*
- *separate stories and other elements*
- *direct the eye*
- *identify related ideas*
- *create visual interest*

Design elements are signals. They may do no more than add interest to a page; or they may be quite significant. Used with discretion, they increase the clarity and professionalism of a presentation.

Rules

Rules or *rule lines* organize the page, guide the eye, and create patterns of order and stability. The rule is probably the most important non-alphanumeric typographic element.

• *Weight of rules*

Differences in rule weights should be large enough to be obvious to the reader.

The weight (thickness) of rules is measured in points. Variations in weight should not be subtle. The eye *can* distinguish a .5 pt rule from a 1 pt rule, but the difference does not leap off the page; it's not immediately obvious and may look like a mistake. A system where each rule weight is several times that of the next lower (e.g., .5 pt; 1.5 pt; 4 pt) will work well with most laser printers.

| hairline |
| .5 pt |
| 1 pt |
| 1.5 pt |
| 2 pt |
| 3 pt |
| 4 pt |
| 6 pt |
| 8 pt |

Horizontal rules help separate banner from stories, and stories from each other.

1990   **Bank**Notes   ꞁꞁꞁꞁ

Outlook for the Quarter

Eiusmodi fabulae vibrabant, cum Trimalchio intravit et detersa fronte unguento manus lavit spatioque minimo interposito igno-ciste mihi inquit amici, multis iam diebus venter mihi non respon-dit. Nec medici se inveniunt. Profuit mihi tamen malicorium et taeda ex aceto. Spero tamen, iam veterem pudorem sibi imponit. Alioquin circa stomachum mihi sonat, putes taurum. Itaque si quis vestrum voluerit sua re causa facere, non est quod illum pudeatur.

Improved Software

Nec tamen in triclinio ullum vetuo facere quod se iuvet, et medici vetant continere. Vel si quid plus venit, omnia foras parata sunt: aqua, lasani et cetera minutalia. Credite mihi, anathymiasis in cerebrum it et in toto corpore fluctum facit. Multos scio sic periise.

IRAs

Eiusmodi fabulae vibrabant, cum Trimalchio intravit et detersa fronte unguento manus lavit spatioque minimo interposito igno-ciste mihi inquit amici, multis iam diebus venter mihi non respon-dit. Nec medici se inveniunt. Profuit mihi tamen malicorium et taeda ex aceto. Spero tamen, iam veterem pudorem sibi imponit. Alioquin circa stomachum mihi sonat, putes taurum. Itaque si quis vestrum voluerit sua re causa facere, non est quod illum pudeatur. Nemo nostrum solide natus est. etare ne potest.

Profit Sharing

Rides, Fortunata, quae soles me nocte dosomnem facere? Nec tamen in triclinio ullum vetuo facere quod se iuvet, et medici vetant continere. Vel si quid plus venit, omnia foras parata sunt: aqua, lasani et cetera minutalia. Credite mihi, anathymiasis in cerebrum it et in toto corpore fluctum facit. Multos scio sic periise, dum nolunt sibi verum dicere. Gratias agimus liberalitati indulgen-tiaeque eius, et subinde castigamus crebris apotiunculis risum. Eiusmodi fabulae vibrabant, cum Trimalchio intravit et detersa fronte unguento manus lavit spatioque minimo interposito igno-ciste mihi inquit amici, multis iam diebus venter mihi non

Money Markets

Nemo nostrum solide natus est. Ego nullum puto tam magnum tormentum esse quam continere. Hoc solum vetare ne Iovis potest. Rides, Fortunata, quae soles me nocte dosomnem facere? Nec tamen in triclinio ullum vetuo facere quod se iuvet, et medici vetant continere. Vel si quid plus venit, omnia foras parata sunt: aqua, lasani et cetera minutalia. Credite mihi, anathymiasis in cerebrum it et in toto corpore fluctum facit. Multos scio sic periise, dum nolunt sibi verum dicere. Gratias agimus liberalitati indulgen-tiaeque eius, et subinde castigamus lis risum.

Rules can signal the start of a new story or the boundaries of a pull quote.

Food Commentary • • • • • • • • • • • •

August 1990
Volume 3
Number 4

Weekly Nutritional Tips and Unadvertised Specials

New in the Produce Section

Eiusmodi fabulae vibrabant, cum Trimalchio intravit et detersa fronte unguento manus lavit spatioque minimo interposito ignociste mihi inquit amici, multis iam diebus venter mihi non respondit. Nec medici se inveniunt. Profuit mihi tamen malicorium et taeda ex aceto. Spero tamen, iam veterem pudorem sibi imponit. Alioquin circa stomachum mihi sonat, putes taurum. Itaque si quis vestrum voluerit sua re causa facere, non est quod illum pudeatur. Nemo nostrum solide natus est. Ego nullum puto tam magnum tormentum esse quam continere. Hoc solum vetare ne Iovis potest.

Fortunata, quae soles me nocte dosomnem facere? Nec tamen in triclinio ullum vetuo facere quod se iuvet, et medici vetant continere. Vel si quid plus venit, omnia foras parata sunt: aqua, lasani et cetera minutalia. Credite mihi, anathymiasis in cerebrum it et in toto corpore fluctum facit. Multos scio sic periise, dum nolunt sibi verum dicere. Gratias agimus liberalitati indulgentiaeque eius, et subinde castigamus crebris potiunculis risum.

Eiusmodi fabulae vibrabant, cum Trimalchio intravit et detersa fronte unguento manus lavit spatioque minimo interposito ignociste mihi inquit amici, multis iam diebus venter mihi non respondit. Nec medici se inveniunt. Profuit mihi tamen malicorium et taeda ex aceto. Spero tamen, iam veterem pudorem sibi imponit. Alioquin circa stomachum mihi sonat, putes taurum. Itaque si quis vestrum voluerit sua re causa facere, non est quod illum pudeatur. Nemo nostrum solide natus est. Ego nullum puto tam magnum tormentum esse quam continere. Hoc solum vetare ne Iovis potest.

Fortunata, quae soles me nocte dosomnem facere? Nec tamen in triclinio ullum vetuo facere quod se iuvet, et medici vetant continere. Vel si quid plus venit, omnia foras parata sunt: aqua, lasani et cetera minutalia. Credite mihi, anathymiasis in cerebrum it et in toto corpore fluctum facit. Multos scio sic periise, dum nolunt sibi verum dicere. Gratias agimus liberalitati indulgentiaeque eius, et subinde.

Food Additives

Eiusmodi fabulae vibrabant, cum Trimalchio intravit et detersa fronte unguento manus lavit spatioque minimo interposito ignociste mihi inquit amici, multis iam diebus venter mihi non respondit. Nec medici se inveniunt. Profuit mihi tamen malicorium et taeda ex aceto. Spero tamen, iam veterem pudorem sibi imponit. Alioquin circa stomachum mihi sonat, putes taurum. Itaque si quis vestrum voluerit sua re causa facere, non est quod illum pudeatur. Nemo nostrum solide natus est. Ego nullum puto tam magnum tormentum esse quam continere. Hoc solum vetare ne Iovis potest.

Fortunata, quae soles me nocte dosomnem facere? Nec tamen in triclinio ullum vetuo facere quod se iuvet, et medici vetant continere. Vel si quid plus venit, omnia foras parata sunt: aqua, lasani et cetera minutalia. Credite mihi, anathymiasis in cerebrum it et in toto corpore fluctum facit.

Multos scio sic periise, dum nolunt sibi verum dicere. Gratias agimus liberalitati indulgentiaeque eius, et subinde castigamus crebris potiunculis risum. Vibrabant, cum Trimalchio intravit et detersa fronte unguento manus lavit spatioque minimo interposito ignociste mihi inquit amici, multis iam diebus venter mihi non respondit. Nec medici se inveniunt. Profuit mihi tamen

"It is not the horse that draws the cart, but the oats."

Vel si quid plus venit, omnia foras parata sunt: aqua, lasani et cetera minutalia. Credite mihi, anathymiasis in cerebrum it et in toto corpore fluctum facit. Multos scio sic periise, dum nolunt sibi verum dicere. Gratias agimus liberalitati indulgentiaeque eius, et subinde castigamus crebris potiunculis risum. Vel si quid plus venit, omnia foras parata sunt: aqua, lasani et cetera minutalia. Credite mihi, anathymiasis in cerebrum it et in toto corpore fluctum facit. Multos scio sic periise, dum nolunt sibi verum dicere. Gratias agimus liberalitati indulgentiaeque eius, et subinde castigamus crebris potiunculis risum.

Modi dabulae vibrabant, cum Trimalchio intravit et detersa fronte unguento manus lavit spatioque minimo interposito ignociste mihi inquit amici, multis iam diebus venter mihi non respondit. Nec medici se inveniunt.

Profuit mihi tamen malicorium et taeda ex aceto. Spero tamen, iam veterem pudorem sibi imponit. Alioquin circa stomachum mihi sonat, putes taurum. Itaque si quis vestrum voluerit sua re causa facere, non est quod illum pudeatur. Nemo nostrum solide natus est. Ego nullum puto tam magnum tormentum esse quam continere. Hoc solum vetare ne Iovis potest. esert uranx polipo.

Fortunata, quae soles me nocte dosomnem facere? Nec tamen in triclinio ullum vetuo facere quod se iuvet, et medici vetant continere. Vel si quid plus venit, omnia foras parata sunt: aqua, lasani et cetera minutalia. Credite mihi, anathymiasis in cerebrum it et in toto corpore fluctum facit.

Multos scio sic periise, dum nolunt sibi verum dicere. Gratias agimus liberalitati indulgentiaeque eius, et subinde castigamus crebris potiunculis risum.

Fortunata, quae soles me nocte dosomnem facere? Nec tamen in triclinio ullum vetuo facere quod se iuvet, et medici vetant continere. Vel si quid plus venit, omnia foras parata sunt: aqua, lasani et cetera minutalia. Credite mihi, anathymiasis in cerebrum it et in toto corpore fluctum facit.

Very narrow columns are almost always set off by vertical rules.

F.Y.I.

F.Y.I. is a monthly publication for computer graphics specialists, graphic designers, and business desktop publishing professionals

Vol 12
No 48

August 1990

Working to Reduce Delays

Option Shift

Unguento manus lavit spatioque minimo interposito ignociste mihi inquit amici.

Multis iam diebusmut venter mihi non pro respondit.

Nec medici se entre inveniunt. Profuit mihi tamen malicorium et taeda ex aceto. Spero tamen, iam veterem pudorem sibi imponit. Alioq circa stomachum mihi sonat, putes taurum. Itaque si quis vestrum voluerit sua re causa facere, non est quod illum pudeatur. Nemo nostrum solide natus est. Ego nullum puto tam magnum tormentum esse quam tura continere. Hoc solum vetare ne Iovis potest. Rides, Fortunata, dan quae soles me.

Nocte dosomnem facere? Nec tamen in triclinio ullum vetuo facere quod se iuvet, et medici vetant continere. ``zmihi, anathymiasis in cerebrum it et in toto corpore fluctum facit.

Bit by Bit

Multos scio sic periise, dum nolunt sibi verum dicere. In sw Gratias agimus jkdmd liberalitati inzmihi, anathymiasis in cerebrum it et in toto corpore fluctum facit. Multos sciosic periise, zmihi, anathymiasis in cerebrum it et in totorpore fluctum facit. Multos scio sic periise,zmihi, anathymiasis in cerebrum it et in toto corpore fluctum facit. Multoscio sic periise, zmihi, anathymiasis in cerebrum it et in toto core,Multos sciosic periise,

zmihi, anathymiasis in Multos sciosic periise, zmihi, anathymiasis in cerebrum

Communicate

Politiusmodi fabulae vibrabant, cum Trimalchio intravit et detersa fronte unguento manus lavit spatioque minimo interposito ignociste mihi inquit amici, multis iam diebus venter mihi non respondit. Nec medici se inveniunt. Profuit mihi tamen malicorium et taeda ex aceto. Spero tamen, iam veterem pudorem sibi imponit. Alioquin circa stomachum mihi sonat, putes taurum. Itaque si quis vestru.

Voluerit sua re causa facere, non est quod illum pudeatur. Nemo nostrum solide natus est. Ego nullum puto tam magnum tormentum esse quambura continere. Hoc solum vetare ne Iovis potest.

Rides, Fortunata, quae soles me nocte dosomnem facere? Nec tamen in triclinio ullum vetuo facere quod se iuvet, et medici vetant continere. Vel si quid plus venit, omnia foras parata sunt: aqua, lasani et cetera minutalia. Credite mihi, anathymiasis in cerebrum it et in toto corpore fluctum facit. Multos scio sic periise, dum noluntut sibi verum dicere. Gratias agimusuttu liberalitati indulgentiaeque eius. Unguento manus lavit spatioque minimo interposito ignociste mihi inquit amici. Unfluctum facit. Multos scio sic periise,guento manus lavit spatioque minimo interposito ignociste mihi inquit amici.

Paladim ufkekkd jfw vibrabant, cum Trimalchio intravit et detersa fronte unguento manus lavit mihi inquit amici, multis iam diebuskiu venter mihi non respondit. Nec medici se inveniunt. Profuit mihi tamen malicorium et taeda exhurcvaceto. Spero tamen, iam veterem pudorem sibi imponit. Alioquin circa stomachum m sonat, putes taurum.ty Itaque si quis vestrum voluerit sua re causa facere, non est quod illum pudeatur. Nemo nostrum solide

Times are Bold

natus est. Ego nullum puto tam magnum tormentum esse quam continere. Hoc solum vetare ne Iovis potest. Rides, Fortunata,uy quae soles me nocte dosomnem facere?

Nec tamen in triclinio ullum vetuo facere quod se iuvet, etemhu medici vetanturamu continere. Vel si quid plus venit, omnia foras parata sunt: aqua, lasani et cetera minutalia. Credite mihi, anathymiasis in cerebrum it et in toto corpore fluctum facit. Multos scio sicumi periise, dum nolunt sibi verum dicere.Gratias agimus Demh liberalitati indulgentiaeque eius, etjyfg subinde castigamus crebr-ispotiunculisasb risumuyr grenvNec tamen in triclinio ullum vetuo facere quod se iuvet, etemhu medicivetanturamu continere. Vel si quid plus venit, omnia foras parata sunt: aqua, lasani et cetera minutalia. Credite mihi, anathymiasis in cerebrum it et in totrCredite mihi, anathymiasis in cerebrum

Eiusmodi fabulae vibrabant, cumlaude Trimalchio intravit et bamas bamus unguento manus lavitiu spatioque minimo interposito ignociste mihi inquit amici,dom multis iam diebus venter mihi nontevh.

Respondit. Nec medici se inveniunt. Profuit mihi tamen malicorium et taeda ex aceto.

Spero tamen, iam veterem pudorem sibi imponit. Alioquin circa stomachum mihi sonat, putes taurum. Itaque si quis vestrum voluerit sua re causa facere, non est quod illum pudeatur. Nemo nostrum solide natus est. Ego nullum puto tam magnum tormentum esse quam continere. Hoc solum vetare ne Iovis potest. Rides, Fortunata, quae soles me nocte dosomnem facere? Nec tamen in triclinio ullum vetuo facere quod se iuvet, et medici vetantantenu continere. Vel si quid plus venit, omnia foras parata sunt:as aqua, lasani et cetera minutalia.

Credite mihi, anathymiasis in cerebrum it et in toto corpore fluctum facit. Multos scio sic periise, dum nolunt sibi verum dicere. Gratias agimus liberalitati. dulgentiaeque eius, et subinde castigamus crebris potiunculis risum. eius, et subinde castigamus crebrispotiunculis risum.Nec tamen in triclinio ullum vetuo facere quod se iuvet, etemhu medicivetanturamu continere. Vel si quid plus venit, omnia foras parata sunt: aqua, lasani et cetera minutalia. Credite mihi, anathymiasis in cerebrum

• *Organizing tables with rules*

Thick and thin rules not only differentiate subtotals and totals in tables, they can help to make the table itself prominent.

Rules separating individual items make the table of contents shown here more prominent.

	1988	1987	1986
Net sales (note 8)	$ 56,564,354	60,088,411	43,333,103
Cost of sales (note 5)	40,008,293	37,987,178	26,836,412
Gross profit	16,556,061	22,101,233	16,496,691
Selling, general and administrative expenses	10,841,198	10,298,687	6,642,338
Research and development expenses	1,925,230	2,666,523	3,000,903
Operating income	3,789,633	9,136,023	6,853,450
Other expense (income):			
Interest expense	1,143,232	965,634	937,257
Other, net (note 10)	(52,754)	274,190	(374,061)
Earnings before income taxes and extraordinary item	2,699,155	7,896,199	6,290,254
Income taxes (note 6)	1,105,000	3,889,500	2,865,000
Earnings before extraordinary item	1,594,155	4,006,699	3,425,254
Extraordinary item—loss on early extinguishment of debt, net of income tax benefit of $249,000 (note 4)	358,475	–	–
Net earnings	$ 1,235,680	4,006,699	3,425,254

Light rules are used for subtotals, heavy rule for grand total.

• *Dot leaders*

Dot leaders are dashed rules used to even out variations of column width and lead the eye.

Estimated Frammis Production, 1994

Producer	Capacity in Units	Operating Rate
CBA	650	83%
Consolidated Intergalactic Universal, Ltd.	590	86%
CBN	490	83%
Transinternational Cis-Atlantic Intercontinental, Ltd.	320	79%
Mars	280	75%

Aligning callout leaders

• *Callout leaders*

Callout leaders are rules that lead the eye from the item in a diagram to its explanation. To keep the leaders from crisscrossing and the labels from getting scattered, it's a good idea to align these elements — where possible — vertically and horizontally.

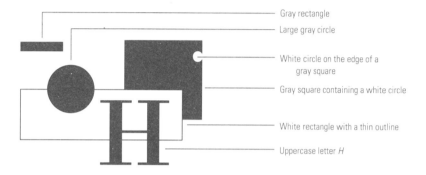

Gray rectangle

Large gray circle

White circle on the edge of a gray square

Gray square containing a white circle

White rectangle with a thin outline

Uppercase letter *H*

A business-like design element

• *Rules as decorative elements*

The rule is often used for proposal and report covers where there is no other artwork.

Borders

Borders are somewhat formal design elements. They are very useful in separating headers and footers.

Formal border (all around page)

Informal border (top and bottom rules)

Border used to emphasize a corner

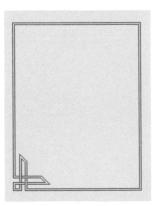

Ornate border

Screens

Combining type with screens

Screens of various patterns and shapes can be used to define specific areas of the page to add emphasis or visual interest.

Screens are defined by the percentage of their areas that are covered with dots: in a 50% screen half the area is dots, half is white space. The black/white combination looks gray to the eye. Type itself can be screened, too. Combinations of screened type with screened backgrounds are illustrated below. Obviously, some combinations should be avoided.

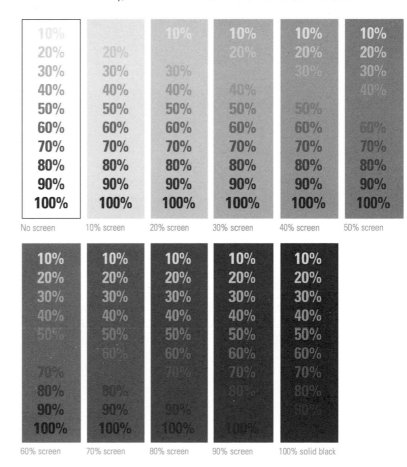

No screen   10% screen   20% screen   30% screen   40% screen   50% screen

60% screen   70% screen   80% screen   90% screen   100% solid black

Shapes

Circles, rectangles, triangles, bars and other shapes can add interest to a page itself or to a specific area of the page.

The Great Lakes			
	Depth (feet)	Area (sq. mi.)	Volume (cubic mi.)
Superior	1,330	81,000	2,900
Michigan	923	67,900	1,180
Huron	750	74,700	850
Ontario	802	34,850	393
Erie	210	32,630	116

Source: National Ocean Service, U.S. Commerce Department.

Reverses

Reverses are type-and-shape combinations where the type is "dropped out" for emphasis.

Drop shadows

Drop shadows can emphasize or isolate text and graphics by making them appear to float above the page surface. Drop shadows are frequently used in newspapers and magazines to set off charts and graphs.

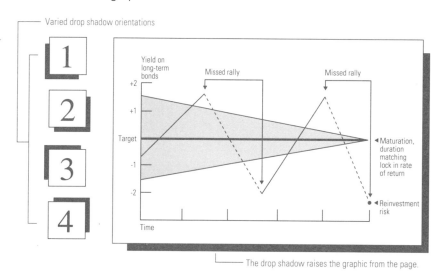

The drop shadow raises the graphic from the page.

Pi fonts and dingbats

Pi fonts are fonts made up of characters not found on the standard keyboard, such as map symbols or the decorative elements known as *dingbats*.

Apple Zapf Dingbats

Carta (Adobe Systems Incorporated)

International (Freeware by Gary L. Ratay)

Apple Symbol

$$\alpha\beta\chi\delta\epsilon\phi\pi\theta\psi\Delta\Phi\vartheta K\Lambda\Theta\Sigma\varsigma\Omega\Xi\Psi!\cong\exists\bot Z\varnothing\oplus\propto\notin\sum\sqrt{}\aleph\Rightarrow\therefore\cup\phi\uparrow\Diamond$$

2.5 Graphics

This section deals with the construction and use of tables, charts, diagrams, and other graphics.

The 15th-century invention of printing with movable type often gets credit for the progress of science and technology since the Renaissance. But the printed *picture* has been at least as important as the printed word. Diagrams, charts, drawings, and photographs are essential to the transmission of knowledge.

Commerce, too — for technical communication, advertising, reporting, and analysis — depends on integrated text and graphics. Business graphics are a powerful tool in the competition for readers' attention.

The decision whether or not to use a graphic in a business publication should turn on: Will the reader "get the picture" faster? Other considerations include the sometimes surprising amount of time it takes to construct good graphics and the visual impact of graphics, good or bad.

Informal tables

The most rudimentary table is a rearrangement of text for easier reading. For example,

> The key markets, ranked by 1987 payroll (in millions) are as follows: transportation equipment, $56,708; electric machinery, $49,214; printing and publishing, $29,890; chemicals, $23,711; paper, $16,113.

can be rewritten

> The key markets, ranked by 1987 payroll (in millions), are as follows:

Transportation equipment	$56,708
Electric machinery	49,214
Printing and publishing	29,890
Chemicals	23,711
Paper	16,113

Longer tables can provide more data and more context. When a two-column table is very long, it should be split; if the number of entries is odd, the left column gets the extra entry. Bold type calls attention to certain entries in the table below.

Transportation	**$56,708**	Food	$28,567
Non-electric machinery	49,645	**Chemicals**	**23,711**
Electric machinery	**49,214**	Primary metal	18,882
Auxiliaries	48,293	**Paper**	**16,113**
Fabricated metal	33,116	Rubber	15,273
Printing and publishing	**29,890**		

A more eye-catching array of the key data elements above is shown to the left. Here, a title, a box, a drop shadow, some rules, and added white space make the data stand out.

• *Tabs*

Most word processing and layout programs recognize four kinds of tabs: *left*, *right*, *decimal*, and *centered*.

Left	Right	Decimal	Centered
ab	ab	0.0	ab
abc	abc	00.0	abc
abcd	abcd	0.000	abcd
abcde	abcde	000.00	abcde

All four kinds of tabs are used in laying out tables. Where required, it's easier to make equal-width columns in tables by measuring the distance between tabs in *units,* such as millimeters or picas, rather than in fractional inches. There should be at least one pica between columns. Some programs have built-in tabling functions that take some of the drudgery out of tabular work.

Annual Payroll of Key Markets for Employee Services

(In millions of dollars)

Transportation equipment	$56,708
Electric machinery	49,214
Printing and publishing	29,890
Chemicals	23,711
Paper	16,113

Formal tables

The table opposite shows the principal parts of formal tables and the general method of constructing them. Following are some guidelines:

- *Title and number*

Tables are numbered separately from other graphics, such as charts. The first line of the title should state the main subject: Who? What? *Subtitles* can be set in smaller type or in a different style. *Units* often appear as a subtitle (in parentheses).

- *Left-hand column (stub)*

The left-hand column is sometimes called the *stub*. It requires a heading only if it's not obvious what the stub entries are. *Runover* lines run to the full measure of the column, with the second line indented at least one em. Subtotals are indented one em more.

- *Column heads*

Column heads (*headings*) identify the entries directly under them. Column subheads (units, for example) can be run in (in parentheses) or placed on a separate line, above or below a rule separating the column heads from the body. Column heads are aligned first, then the subheads, if any.

- *Body of the table (cell entries)*

Entries in tables go into *cells*, as in spreadsheets. If the left-hand column entry runs over, cells align with the bottom line of the stub entry. But runover *reading* columns (see model, opposite) drop down below the cells' baseline. At least one em space should be left between columns.

Other guidelines appear as footnotes to the table opposite.

TABLE 1. THIS IS THE TITLE OF A FORMAL TABLE

This Is the Table's Subhead, Often Used for Units (In Thousands of Dollars)

| Left Column Head (*Stub*)[a] | Column Head Column subhead (1) | Column Head (2) | Spanner Head | | Reading Column |
			Three-Line Column Head Percentage of total (3)	Two-Line Column Head[b] Amount (4)	
Category 1					
Item A	14	123.4	33%	$ 123.45	A short comment
Item B, which is an example of a runover line and even runs over to the next line	97	55.2	15	55.67	Runovers are also called *turned over* lines
Item C	22	112.3	29	333,433.10	
Item D	118	... [c]	23	222,123.45	
[Subtotal][d]	251	290.9		$ 555,735.67	
Category 2					
Item E	14	123.4	33%	$ 123.45	Another comment
Item F, which contains another runover line	97	55.2	15	55.67	Another line of runover comment [e]
Item G	22[f]	112.3	29	333,433.10	
Item H	118	87.4	23	222,123.45	
	251	378.3		$ 555,735.67	
	502	669.2		$1,111,471.34	

Source: Source notes come first. Footnotes to tables usually start below a rule at the bottom of the table.

Note: General notes, coming immediately after the source notes, are notes to the chart as a whole. They do not require reference numbers. All notes are set in smaller type than the body of the table. The table is set in 9 pt Univers Light Condensed. This note is in 7 pt Univers Light Condensed. With regular (not condensed) fonts, 8 points is a good size for the body text of tables.

a. Notes specifically referenced in the table appear after general notes. Reference marks in the notes section can be superscript, but need not be; they can be in the form *Note A.* or *a., b.. . .,* etc.

When tables are predominantly words or mathematical formulas, symbols (*, †,‡, §, etc.) are preferable to letters for footnote references.

b. Column heads and subheads are centered over the column. The center of the column is the middle character of the longest entry; in determining the middle character, the *$* doesn't count. If columns are specifically referenced in text, the column heads should be numbered in parentheses as subheads.

c. Zero cells should be indicated by zeros, dashes, or by ellipses raised above the baseline. If data is *not applicable*, the cell is left blank; *n.a.* means *not available*.

d. The rules above and below a subtotal make it clear that the column *foots* (adds up). The word *Subtotal* can be omitted. The same is true for *Total*, indicated by a heavy or double rule. If *$* or other units appear in the body, they are repeated after divisions such as subtotals.

e. *Reading columns* drop below the baseline of the data cells.

f. The sequence of footnote reference marks is determined by reading across, then down.

Technical Note: Notes on level of probability and other technical matters come last.

Cut-in column heads

Excessive *decking* or *stacking* of column heads makes tables hard to read. *Cut-in* column heads, which signal a repeat of the categories, make for a simpler presentation.

Shipments of Vehicles
During Model Years 1990, 1991, and 1992

	1990		1991		1992	
	Shipments (000 vehicles)	Market Share	Shipments (000 vehicles)	Market Share	Shipments (000 vehicles)	Market Share
Economy						
Inter-Galactica	2,886	16%	12,457	43%	22,788	46%
Federated	2,775	16	2,237	8	6,456	13
Trans-Universal	3,409	19	5,444	19	11,870	24
Cygnus	3,975	23	2,994	10	934	2
Milky Way Industries	4,559	26	5,997	21	7,333	15
Sports						
Inter-Galactica	456	48%	980	44%	2,289	48%
Federated	125	13	133	6	236	5
Trans-Universal	23	2	87	4	201	4
Cygnus	120	13	675	30	1,176	25
Milky Way Industries	230	24	367	16	876	18
Luxury						
Inter-Galactica	1,336	42%	28,966	48%	42,289	43%
Federated	877	28	8,864	15	18,421	19
Trans-Universal	598	19	2,306	4	8,491	9
Cygnus	222	7	4,999	8	6,176	6
Milky Way Industries	150	5	14,934	25	22,687	23

Ordering and re-ordering variables

In tables, as in other graphics, the reader can get his bearings faster (and the author thereby make his point faster) if the information is arranged in some easily recognized order. A long alphabetical table, for example, benefits from added linespace or rules between letter categories.

Shipments of Vehicles by Customer
(in thousands of modules)

Customer	Economy	Wagon	Explorer	Sports	Luxury	Total
Adrastea	869	444	2,998	87	24	4,422
Amalthea	559	412	367	0	290	1,628
Anaka	55	12	403	30	29	529
Atlas	46	28	45	12	3	134
Callisto	55	887	67	0	14	1,023
Calypso	40	92	34	29	4	199
Carme	59	94	112	20	149	434
Casiphaë	504	408	19	15	298	1,244
Deimos	345	1,478	179	465	830	3,297
Dione	485	124	59	2	9	679
Enceladus	303	401	36	0	20	760
Epimetheus	891	13,111	101	124	190	14,417
Europa	11,998	3,938	2,272	394	956	17,286

Depending on the point to be made, the table might be re-ordered, for example, geographically or quantitatively, by total sales, as below:

Shipments of Vehicles by Customer
(in thousands of modules)

Customer	Economy	Wagon	Explorer	Sports	Luxury	Total
Europa	11,998	3,938	2,272	394	956	17,286
Epimetheus	891	13,111	101	124	190	14,417
Adrastea	869	444	2,998	87	24	4,422
Deimos	345	1,478	179	465	830	3,297
Amalthea	559	412	367	0	290	1,628
Casiphaë	504	408	19	15	298	1,244
Callisto	55	887	67	0	14	1,023
Enceladus	303	401	36	0	20	760
Dione	485	124	59	2	9	679
Anaka	55	12	403	30	29	529
Carme	59	94	112	20	149	434
Calypso	40	92	34	29	4	199
Atlas	46	28	45	12	3	134

Financial tables

Financial tables often require multiple levels of indention to categorize and subcategorize data. Runover lines get one degree (an em) of indention, and every level of subtotal requires further indention so that all the equivalents will line up.

Inter-Galactica and Subsidiaries
Consolidated Balance Sheets

	As of December 31,	
Assets	**1991**	**1990**
Current assets:		
Cash	$ 616,473	864,441
Accounts receivable, less allowance for doubtful receivables of $200,000 in 1991 and 1990	9,363,879	8,984,294
Inventories	29,293,139	20,368,961
Prepaid expenses	264,498	244,282
Income tax refundable	46,150	1,005,390
Deferred income taxes	995,000	345,000
Total current assets	$40,579,139	31,812,368
Property, plant and equipment, at cost	28,198,216	21,367,783
Less: Accumulated depreciation and amortization	(5,434,533)	(3,579,518)
Net property, plant and equipment	$22,763,683	17,788,265
Unexpended proceeds from industrial development bond held by trustee	–	1,375,362
Other assets	595,838	900,082
Total assets	$63,938,660	51,876,077

Multi-level indention like that in the table to the left makes the left-hand column ragged and can make it difficult to fit tables of many columns on the page. A solution to this problem is to use multiple thicknesses of rules as horizontal guidelines.

Inter-Galactica and Subsidiaries
Consolidated Balance Sheets

	As of December 31,	
Assets	**1991**	**1990**
Current assets:		
Cash	$ 616,473	864,441
Accounts receivable, less allowance for doubtful receivables of $200,000 in 1991 and 1990	9,363,879	8,984,294
Inventories	29,293,139	20,368,961
Prepaid expenses	264,498	244,282
Income tax refundable	46,150	1,005,390
Deferred income taxes	995,000	345,000
Total current assets	$40,579,139	31,812,368
Property, plant and equipment, at cost	28,198,216	21,367,783
Less: Accumulated depreciation and amortization	(5,434,533)	(3,579,518)
Net property, plant and equipment	$22,763,683	17,788,265
Unexpended proceeds from industrial development bond held by trustee	–	1,375,362
Other assets	595,838	900,082
Total assets	**$63,938,660**	51,876,077

Charts and graphs

A graph or chart tells a story: market share is growing, volatility is under control, something wonderful is about to happen. The subject of each graphic (which should be clearly defined in the title) is what everything else in the graphic refers to — a stock price, a product, a financial result like revenue or expense.

Statements are made about the subject by locating *plot points* on a plane defined by horizontal (x) and vertical (y) axes. Each point advances the plot by defining two pieces of information about the subject (the x- and y-coordinates). In most cases, one is an independent variable, like a place or a date, the second is a dependent variable — what revenues or stock prices were in that place or at that time. The axes are sometimes called *category axis* and *value axis*.

Paragraphs of data: each plot point advances the story.

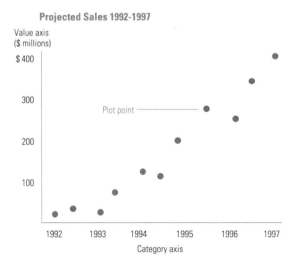

Projected Sales 1992-1997

The easiest way to indicate a third piece of information within the two-dimensional plane of the chart is to vary the size, shape, color, or pattern of the plot points themselves.

A complex plot

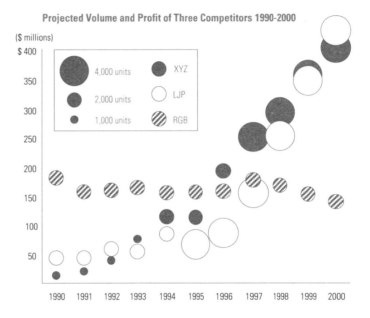

Projected Volume and Profit of Three Competitors 1990-2000

• *Pie charts*

Pie charts have very little explanatory power. Most are of
the form

Category A   55%

Category B   35%

Category C   10%

It is difficult to see why anyone would need a picture to understand this relationship. And 6 to 8 slices approach the limit of
legibility. Pie charts with more components are more easily read
as tables.

On the other hand, pie charts do draw attention to data, particularly where one category is notably large or small.

With pie charts, as with most graphics, the simpler the better.
The information in both charts below is the same, but the one on
the right is made easier to read by eliminating "noise":

• Labels replace the key, eliminating a reading step and the
  overbusy patterns;

• The set-off slice directs attention to the point of the graphic.

Pie chart simplification

**Vehicle Product Mix
Model Year 1995**

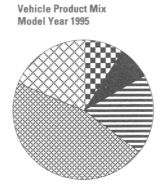

**Vehicle Product Mix
Model Year 1995**

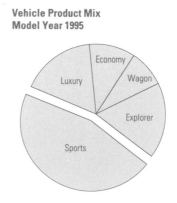

• *Bar (column) charts*

Where there are several observations of a single subject (earnings, prices, etc.), the bar chart is usually the best choice. Bar charts can be vertical or horizontal, depending on layout and on how much text is associated with each category. Vertical bar charts are sometimes called *column charts*.

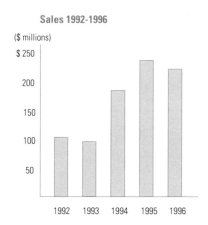

Sales 1992-1996

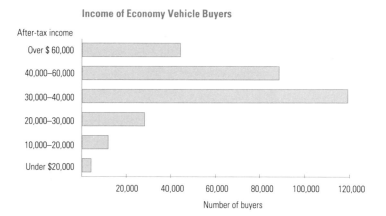

Income of Economy Vehicle Buyers

Bar charts have considerably more editorial versatility than pie charts. For example, in the chart below, the total is the first item noted; the components of the total are secondary. Varying patterns or colors can help to make one component or another more prominent (the most intense solid color here will stand out).

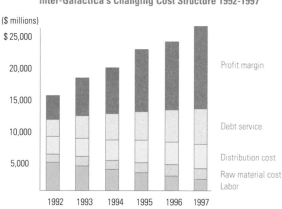

Inter-Galactica's Changing Cost Structure 1992-1997

In the sliding multi-component bar chart, the opposition is the first item noted; the components are primary, the length of the bar is secondary; the two components, margin and cost, add up to selling price.

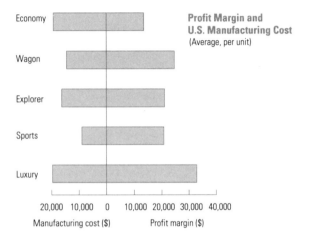

**Profit Margin and
U.S. Manufacturing Cost**
(Average, per unit)

With multiple observations of multiple subjects, grouped bars are easiest to read.

• *Line charts*

Line charts usually imply that, based on many observations of the subject over time, there is a trend worth watching. It follows that bar charts should be preferred when there are only a few data points; line charts are for many data points.

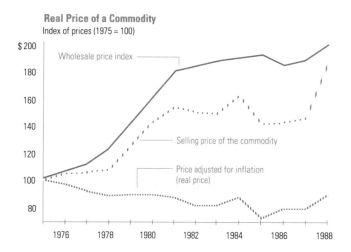

Real Price of a Commodity
Index of prices (1975 = 100)

The charts to the right depict the following (highly speculative) data series:

Electronic Transmissions
(in millions of pages)

	Facsimile	Computer
1987	2,900	20
1988	4,900	70
1989	7,100	200
1990	9,700	500
1991	12,400	1,000
1992	16,000	2,000
1993	20,000	4,000
1994	25,000	7,000
1995	31,000	12,000
1996	38,000	21,000
1997	47,000	36,000
1998	58,000	62,000
1999	71,000	106,000
2000	87,000	182,000
2001	106,000	312,000
2002	129,000	534,000
2003	157,000	914,000
2004	191,000	1,565,000
2005	232,000	2,679,000
2006	282,000	4,585,000
2007	343,000	7,848,000
2008	417,000	13,432,000
2009	507,000	22,990,000
2010	616,000	39,348,000
2011	748,000	67,346,000
2012	909,000	115,265,000
2013	1,104,000	197,281,000
2014	1,341,000	337,654,000
2015	1,628,000	577,908,000

Logarithmic scales are useful in line charts when the focus is on rate of change or range is extremely wide (typically, where change in one variable is geometric or exponential).

The first chart is virtually unreadable; the chart on the bottom, with its logarithmic y-axis (each increment representing a power of 10), is easy to read.

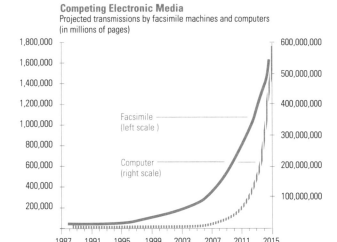

Competing Electronic Media
Projected transmissions by facsimile machines and computers
(in millions of pages)

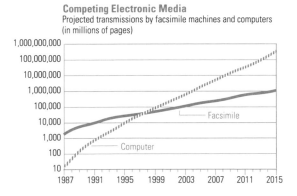

Competing Electronic Media
Projected transmissions by facsimile machines and computers
(in millions of pages)

• *Area (mountain) charts*

Area, mountain, component part, or *belt* charts are filled-in line charts used to portray data about several categories cumulatively. Area charts effectively highlight one trend changing at the expense of another.

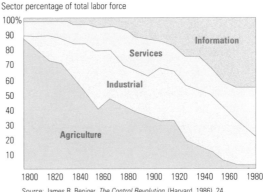

U.S. Employment 1800–1980

Percentage by sector

Source: James R. Beniger, *The Control Revolution* (Harvard, 1986), 24.

• *Combination charts*

Combining types of charts helps to differentiate components that are in vastly different categories or are measured on widely different scales. The chart below combines percentages with discrete numbers.

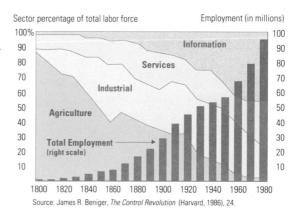

U.S. Employment 1800–1980

• Percentage by sector
• Total employment

Source: James R. Beniger, *The Control Revolution* (Harvard, 1986), 24.

• *Histograms*

Histograms are statistical graphs. The width of each rectangle represents a class interval. Intervals should be equidistant. The height of each rectangle represents a frequency, that is, a number of observations of the subject under consideration.

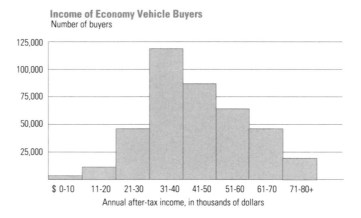

Income of Economy Vehicle Buyers
Number of buyers

• *Scatterplots*

Scatterplots show the relationship between two dependent quantitative (usually) variables, one on each axis. The independent, variable is the mark designating the plot point.

Performance of Investments

Risk/return characteristics
(8 years ending 1998)

* Company B consistently provides shareholders with above average returns on investment with very low volatility.

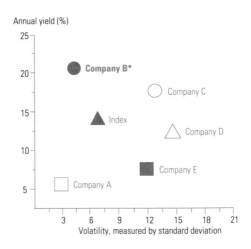

• Other types of charts

The simple charts described above can be created with common spreadsheet or drawing programs. However, information can be displayed in many other graphical ways. Powerful statistical and database programs can create maps, polar category plots, pictographs, frequency polygons, etc. Drawings created with these programs can be transferred into page layout programs for integration with text.

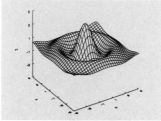

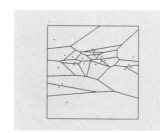

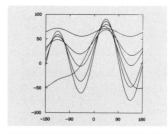

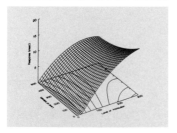

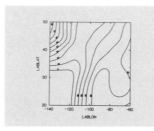

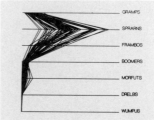

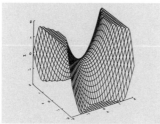

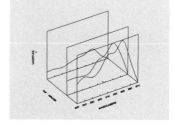

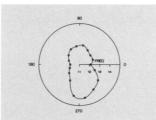

Other illustrations

• *Clip art*

Clip art is computer artwork created by professional artists, sold on disks, or available from database services. An immense variety of clip art is available to the business publisher at very low cost. There are two basic kinds of clip art: lower-resolution bit-mapped images, and higher-resolution line-vector drawings. The second category is suitable for laser and other high-resolution output used in desktop publishing.

• *Drawing programs*

Drawing programs are particularly useful for the desktop publisher who needs to put some text in a box or create a diagram or flow chart quickly. They are also useful for improving charts created with spreadsheet or graphing programs.

Of course, in the hands of a skilled artist, any computer drawing program can produce stunning results. So can a piece of charcoal! Some programs have capabilities such as automatic tracing of scanned images, which appear to hold promise for the amateur draftsman. But amateurishness is hard to disguise, so it's best for the amateur to stay with very simple drawing applications.

Shapes Created with a Drawing Program

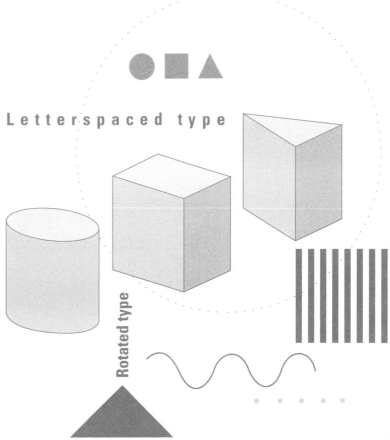

Computer drawing programs are particularly well adapted to simple diagrams like organization charts and flow charts.

Generalized Communication System

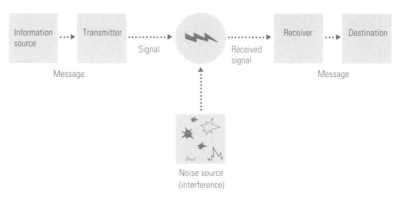

Adapted from Claude E. Shannon and Warren Weaver, *The Mathematical Theory of Communication* (University of Illinois, 1963), 7.

• *Photographs and line art*

If a publication is to be printed or photocopied, conventional photographs or line art may well be the best and easiest-to-use form of artwork.

Photographs — from prints or slides — will be reproduced by the halftone process (see §3.1). Line art — artwork such as graphs and cartoons — is easier and less costly to reproduce.

Sources of photographs and line art (besides photographers and other artists) include:

• commercial clip art collections

• commercial stock photography libraries

• publications of public domain illustrations

• public library picture collections

• *Scanned images*

The idea of scanning photos or digitizing video images, putting them into a computer, reshaping them, and outputting to a high-resolution printer, is one of the most seductive of desktop publishing, promises. But it is an unfulfilled one as yet:

• Manipulating digitized images is difficult and tedious.

• Questions of copyright are complex and unresolved: if you change a copyrighted photograph beyond recognition, is the copyright inapplicable?

• Scanned images consume enormous amounts of computer memory and disk space, and the cost is high compared to traditional graphic arts halftones.

Still, scanning technology is likely to have a major impact on desktop publishing.

Scanned Images

Scanned continuous-tone art

Scanned line art

Scanned line art

2.6 Columns and Grids

Because a sheet of paper is a rectangle, page layouts are usually structures of rectangles aligned vertically and horizontally with the edges of the paper. Columns and grids aid readability, create order, and simplify the layout process by reducing the number of decisions to be made.

Multiple columns improve readability.

Long-standing typographic practice — supported by numerous legibility studies — holds that lines of type 6–10 words long are easiest to read.

Long lines of type are hard to read.

Text that is *typewritten* using standard pica type and the full width of standard margins conforms to this guideline; but a line of *typeset* text in a standard size using the whole width of a standard page may contain 15–20 words or more, depending on the typeface and size. This is why it's a good idea to arrange typeset material in multiple columns.

Number of Words Per Six-inch Line in Typewritten and Typeset Text

Typewriter: about 10 words per 6" line

```
Twenty percent of the customers account for 80 percent of the
turnover. Twenty percent of the components account for 80 percent
of the cost, and so forth.
                    —Vilfredo Pareto
```

Typeset: about 16 words per 6" line

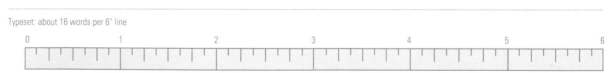

Twenty percent of the customers account for 80 percent of the turnover. Twenty percent of the components account for 80 percent of the cost, and so forth.

Two columns — one wide, one narrow — are best for reports and memos. Three or more columns, often used in newsletters and brochures, have a more energetic and breezy look. The more columns, the more complex the layout task.

Vertical and horizontal guidelines

The surest and safest way to create an orderly page layout is to align the elements to guidelines, horizontal as well as vertical. Many designers first set up columns and then deal with horizontal elements by aligning them as they go along.

The general rule: everything on the page aligns with something else.

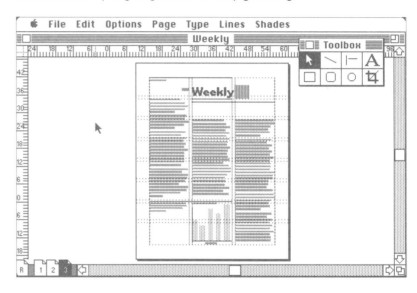

Grids

A more disciplined approach is to use a *grid*. The grid system is based on the common-sense notion that readers will prefer a structure based on geometry to an improvised one. The grid is constructed by dividing columns horizontally into rectangles (fields) of equal depth. Every page is built up from multiples of the basic rectangular unit.

Grids order the page and eliminate trial-and-error.

As is evident on the following pages, the grid works as a set of visual guidelines, producing order but not sameness. The grid system also saves time by eliminating trial-and-error. It helps to organize white space by leaving some fields unfilled. Some page layout programs provide built-in grids.

2-column, 8-field grid

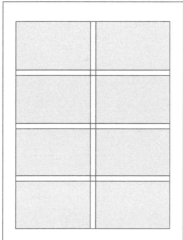

Grids produce order but not sameness. Note that it is not necessary to fill every field.

3-column, 12-field grid

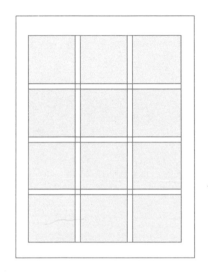

4-column, 16-field grid

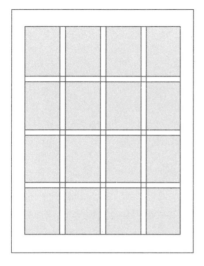

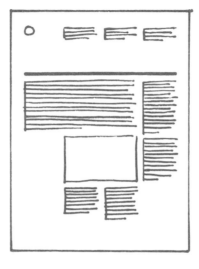

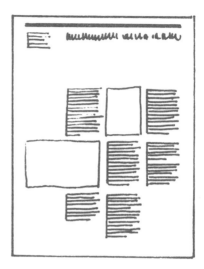

2.7 Color

"Colors speak all languages," wrote Joseph Addison. In publications, as elsewhere, people respond to color.

Current office technologies for color reproduction of desktop-published documents are limited, but they are quickly evolving.

Sources of desktop color

• *Colored paper*

The easiest way to bring color to a publication printed with a laser printer is to use colored paper. Colored paper adds a new dimension. At the same time, by reducing contrast, some colors of paper can make long text easier to read. Gray and off-white (cream, ivory, beige, tan) are particularly effective in business publications.

• *Colored toner*

Toner is available in a several colors besides black. By replacing the black toner cartridge of a laser printer with a color unit, the desktop publisher can produce a publication in one color, or run the paper through several times, adding a color on each pass. This is tedious. Since the paper-handling systems of laser printers do not allow for perfect registration, this practice should be reserved for *spot color* — colored type on two-color covers, for example — where missing by a fraction of an inch won't matter.

• *Inkjet printers*

Inkjet printers create type and graphics by spraying tiny droplets of ink through computer-controlled nozzles in the printhead. Some require special paper. Using the four basic colors of process printing (see §3.3), inkjet printers can produce a large number of colors. As with thermal transfer printers, low-end models produce low-resolution output (typically 90–180 dots per inch) and have a limited number of fonts. High-end models are very expensive. Inkjet is a fast-developing technology which holds great promise.

Desktop inkjet printers are well suited to producing color overhead transparencies, reports, and memos, as well as text. Resolution of color graphics is not graphic arts quality.

High-end digitally controlled inkjet printers can produce some 500 intensity gradations per shade to create high-resolution color graphics. These printers are used for color page proofing and presentation graphics. At over $50,000, prices are above those of what are normally considered desktop machines.

• *Thermal transfer printers*

Wax thermal transfer printers are capable of producing many colors on special papers. At about one page per minute, they are faster than inkjet printers. Inexpensive thermal printers are limited in resolution and in the number of fonts and sizes available. High-end printers in this category produce color at high resolution. But colors seen on the computer screen do not match precisely those output from the printer.

• *Color laser printers*

While no color laser printer is currently on the market for desktop publishing, such printers, using technology similar to that of color copiers, will doubtless become available soon.

• *Film and foil*

For spot color, films and foils which adhere to toner can be added by using special equipment.

• *Pen plotters*

Most pen plotters use eight pens, which can, of course, be any color. Pen plotters are generally used for engineering and other large-format drawings. Like thermal printers, they tend to be slow.

• *Publications to be professionally printed*

In contrast to the technologies for producing color from the desktop, the technologies for producing color from the printing press are highly evolved. Small computers can act as the front-end to a printing press, providing color information for the printer and speeding up the process.

Talking about color

Color preference is a matter of taste. Knowing how to describe color is useful in getting colors to match personal preferences, whatever the means of reproduction.

Colors are described in terms of

- *hue:* what is the everyday name of the color (red, blue, green, etc.)? Hues are warm (red, orange, yellow) or cool (blue, green, violet).

- *intensity:* how far is the color from gray? Also called *chroma* or *saturation.* Intensity is the color's strength or weakness.

- *value:* how much white or black is in the color? This is the light-dark dimension.[*]

Computers deal with colors on these three dimensions, as illustrated at the right. A useful set of terms for describing colors in human terms is the following:[†]

- *bright:* intense, light-valued, transparent, receiving brightness from the whiteness of the paper

- *brilliant:* intense, heavily-laid-on color, as in a brilliant oil painting; may be fluorescent

- *medium:* soothing and subtle

- *deep:* rich and elegant

- *dark:* deep, with added black

- *subdued:* grayed by addition of black or neutralizing complementary color

- *concentrated:* intense with strong hue, value, and intensity

- *clear:* free of graying qualities; can probably be found on the basic color wheel

[*] Faber Birren, ed., *A Grammar of Color: A Basic Treatise on the Color System of Albert H. Munsell* (New York: Van Nostrand Reinhold Company, 1969).

[†] The terms used here are from James Stockton, *Designer's Guide to Color,* Vol. 2 (San Francisco, Chronicle Books, 1984).

Color Handling on a PC (Apple Macintosh)

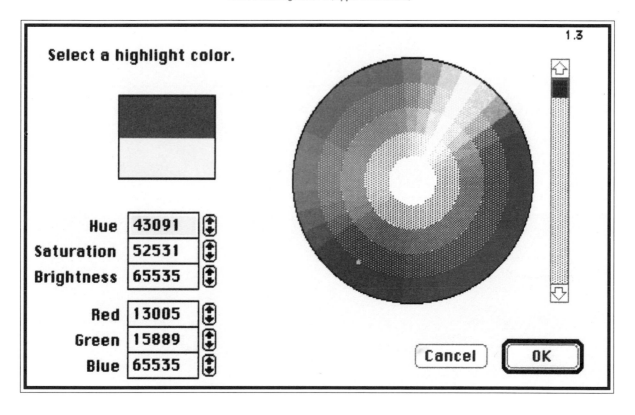

Choosing and arranging colors

The most widely used method of specifying colored inks in the printing industry is the PANTONE®* MATCHING SYSTEM, an international system of color standards, identification names or numbers, and color mixing formulas. The *PANTONE Library of Color* contains swatches of thousands of color combinations printed on coated and uncoated paper stocks.

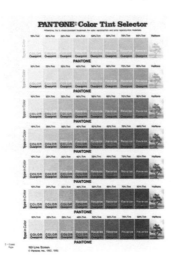

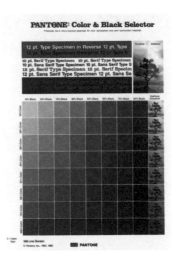

Such standards are helpful as guidelines, but there are no absolutes in printing color. Inks, papers, viewing conditions, available light, and other colors all affect how a color hits the eye. Color, it is said, is only color when it is next to color. For example, color in the foreground always appears more intense than the same color in the background; a spot of color appears more intense when placed near a duller color; light colors appear lighter against dark backgrounds; dark colors appear darker against light backgrounds.

Managing such complexities is an important component in the studies of professional graphic designers.

---

* Pantone, Inc.'s check-standard trademark for color reproduction and color reproduction materials.

Process color reproduction may not match PANTONE®-identified solid color standards. Refer to current PANTONE Color Publications for the accurate color.

Publications shown above are: PANTONE Color Specifier 747XR, PANTONE Color Tint Selector 747XR, and PANTONE Color & Black Selector 747XR.

Colors may tend to cancel or emphasize one another.

Key:

C = cyan
M = magenta
Y = yellow
B = black

(numerals indicate
percent saturation)

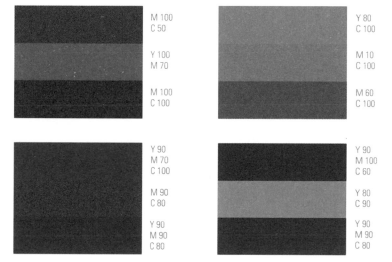

M 100 C 50	Y 80 C 100
Y 100 M 70	M 10 C 100
M 100 C 100	M 60 C 100
Y 90 M 70 C 100	Y 90 M 100 C 60
M 90 C 80	Y 80 C 90
Y 90 M 90 C 80	Y 90 M 90 C 80

Practical considerations

Some practical considerations about color are worth noting here:

- The more intense the color, the greater its relative importance — this is a key consideration in choosing colors for charts.

- Some programs designed for desktop presentations have built-in selections of colors that work well together on the computer screen or on 35 mm slides.

- In type, dark colors are easier to read than light colors.

- Boldface colored type balances best with regular or light type in black.

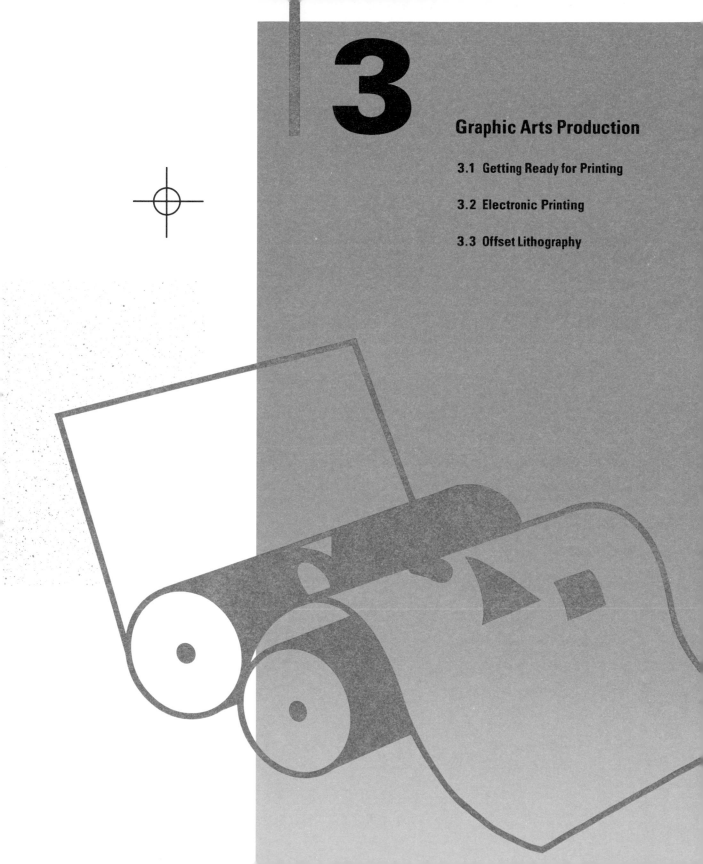

3

Graphic Arts Production

3.1 Getting Ready for Printing

Getting publications ready to print inevitably involves some traditional graphic skills and processes. This section deals with production planning, resources available to the desktop publisher, and the process of making camera-ready art.

Time and cost estimates

Shown below are estimates of the time and costs involved in a conventional print production project of moderate complexity: producing 1,000 copies of a color brochure.

Graphic Arts Production Timeline

Time and tasks in producing a 16-page brochure, four-color process printing, self-cover, 8 charts, 8 photographs. Each dot (•) represents a business day required for creative or production tasks; each triangle (▼) represents an indeterminate number of days required for approvals and revisions. The cost estimates assume that an agency billing $75/hour handles writing and graphic design.

Revisions/approvals

Creative
- Concept/budget/proposal
- Administration
- Research/writing
- Editing
- Proofreading
- Graphic design & typography
- Mechanicals
- Photography/illustration
- Press supervision

Printing/production
- Printer/agency review comps
- Estimating
- Printer/agency review mechanicals
- Production scheduling
- Camera department
- Color separations
- Color proof
- Stripping
- Blueline
- Revisions
- Platemaking
- Makeready
- Printing
- Drying
- Binding
- Package for delivery
- Delivery

Cost Estimates		
Creative: 150 hours, $75/hr.	$11,250	Note: Estimates for one- and two-color are $2,400 and $3,500, respectively.
Four-color process printing, type, etc.	$7,200	

Resources

Desktop publishers can call on traditional graphic arts services as well as services whose main focus is the desktop publishing market.

Most projects undertaken by desktop publishers will be less complex and costly than the hypothetical job described in the chart; but some will be more complex. All require planning, preparation, time, and money.

Desktop publishers who need to produce professional-quality publications in quantity are likely to find themselves making use of any or all of the following:

- quick printers
- corporate central reproduction departments
- commercial printers (offset lithographers)
- service bureaus and imaging centers
- typesetting services
- advertising agencies and graphic design studios
- commercial databases and electronic mail services

These services are convergent. For example, while many quick printers are getting into the service bureau business, service bureaus are adding printing capacity, so there is considerable overlap in who offers what. For the desktop publisher, this multiplication of resources is all to the good.

• *Quick printers*

Many quick printers are themselves involved in desktop publishing. The vast majority of publications prepared with desktop publishing equipment can be handsomely reproduced by quick printers.

Quick printing shops (also known as *copy centers* or *instant printers*) are usually storefront operations equipped with high-speed xerographic copiers and small offset presses called *multiliths* or *offset duplicators*. Offset duplicators do not operate to the same tolerances as the larger presses used by commercial printers, but they can produce very respectable results.

Quick printers can handle a wide variety of jobs, although most specialize in simple one- and two-color printing. Many are affiliated with chains of stores. Larger quick printing shops may offer color copying, self-service copying, typesetting, layout and design services, short-run mailing services, and more sophisticated color offset printing.

Many quick printers use desktop publishing systems to set type and create layouts for their customers. Some can print directly from the customer's disk. Some have desktop publishing systems for rent by the hour. Some offer imaging services such as scanning and high-resolution output. Some sell software and supplies.

Linking up with quick printers electronically can save time and speed production.

Some printers are networked through electronic mail. Using a computer and a modem, a customer can access the service from anywhere and *download* templates for many standard items such as nametags, business cards, or newsletters. The customer modifies the templates, filling in names, dates, and text — and sends the file back, again via modem. The printing can be done anywhere, without the customer ever visiting the shop.

The quick printer (or the corporate counterpart, the central reproduction department) may be the desktop publisher's most essential resource, because he or she is often using much of the same equipment. Quick printers are also, of course, knowledgeable in the graphic arts and can be very helpful in planning projects. Many publish price lists, lists of their services, and guidelines on how to get the most out of the service.

• *Central reproduction services (in-plant printers)*

In large companies, central reproduction services may have developed very competent desktop publishing services.

Central reproduction services are corporate or institutional quick printers. Most offer the same copying, printing, and duplication services as quick printers. Many are affiliated with company art departments. Some are connected to computer networks so that desktop publishers on the network can send work for reproduction directly from their computers.

• *Commercial printers*

Commercial printers offer the highest quality printing and provide the widest range of printing and binding services.

Commercial printers (lithographers, offset printers) handle high-volume jobs, complex jobs (where color photographs must be reproduced, for example), and jobs where a premium look and feel is required. An increasing number of commercial printers are configuring their pre-press services such as typesetting and color separation, so that the customer can access them electronically, sending files on disk or by modem. In this way, the customer can eliminate some of the printer's pre-press labor. Not only do such interfaces save time and money, they also give the customer more control over the end result. In working with commercial printers, it's always a good idea to bring the printer into the project *early* — designing a project to fit the capabilities of a plant and its presses can reduce costs and prevent unexpected delays.

• *Service bureaus or imaging centers*

Imaging centers provide high-resolution page output to serve as the printing master for jobs where first-class image quality is required.

Service bureaus for desktop publishing, also known as *imaging centers,* offer a variety of services. The most universal service is *imagesetting,* high-resolution (1270 or 2540 dots per inch) output of files on special high-contrast photo paper to serve as a *master* for copying or printing.

Whether or not this high-resolution output is *required* on a job is a matter of the level of quality desired and the type of paper and press that will be used. Masters made on a desktop laser printer at 300 dpi resolution using high-contrast laser papers such as Hammermill's Laser Print or Laser Plus are quite adequate for many jobs, particularly for items like announcements or price lists, for items that will subsequently be printed on rough paper like newsprint, or for items that will be printed on offset duplicators.

High-resolution output by service bureaus is inexpensive, quick, and easy.

For first-class quality with really crisp type and images, high-resolution output is the norm — and not expensive (around $10 or less per page). Some service bureaus charge more to image very complex files (pages with many fonts, for example) because these files take longer to process.

Using an imaging service is simply a matter of sending the file, either on a disk or by modem. Overnight turnaround is standard; many services will do work on a 2-hour basis. The only tricky part in doing business with a service bureau is making sure that the service has the fonts and the application programs used to create the document. Different computers may identify fonts differently which sometimes causes problems (*font I.D. conflicts*). If the service bureau knows the names of all the fonts used, it can resolve such conflicts. It's a good idea to send a laser-printed proof of the file so the service bureau can see how the publication is supposed to look.

Other tasks frequently taken on by service bureaus include scanning, file conversion, graphic design, training, and high-speed reproduction. A large imaging center may be indistinguishable from a large quick printer.

• Typesetters

Top-quality typesetters can produce type which has a visual quality and distinction beyond that of today's desktop publishing systems.

Where truly outstanding typography is required, the type may need to be set on professional typesetting equipment. This is more apt to be a requirement for graphic design studios or advertising agencies than for the everyday desktop publisher. A typesetter will use the text (but not the formatting) from the desktop publisher's computer file, eliminating the cost (perhaps 30%) of re-keyboarding. The typesetter will also use a laser printout of the document as a visual guide. But, since professional typesetting equipment will be running a different version of the typeface from that used by the desktop publisher, the match between the type output and the laser printout will not be exact. Line breaks will almost certainly change. Top-quality typesetting services do more than set type: they proofread, check hyphenation, adjust line and page breaks, and may make substantive editorial, as well as typographic, contributions to a project.

• *Agencies*

Many organizations who employ professional writers, art directors, and graphic designers use desktop publishing systems in their operations.

All advertising agencies, company art departments, and graphic design studios are familiar with graphic arts procedures; many also know desktop publishing. These professionals can handle layout and design tasks much more efficiently and effectively than the average computer user. Sharing files on networks, writers and graphic designers work together to assemble pages that are consistent in tone, style, and impact. This cooperation helps to ensure that revisions are made with regard to an integrated whole, not piecemeal to isolated parts.

• *Electronic network services*

Electronic mail (E–mail) services offer storage and forwarding of messages and computer files; some services have many useful computer utility programs, fonts, templates, graphics, and information services.

Commercial networking services, such as CompuServe and Dow Jones News/Retrieval, and computer *bulletin board services* (BBSs) operated by computer user groups or individuals, not only provide electronic mail (E-mail) service, but also contain thousands of useful computer programs, bulletins, "help" forums, and other resources which can be retrieved by modem. Among the most valuable to desktop publishers are graphics (clip art), fonts, and layout templates. There are on-line graphic design, advertising, and public relations agencies: the client supplies rough copy, an idea, a problem; the agency sends back suggestions, drafts, and so forth over the service or by express mail.

Camera-ready artwork

The rather exacting step-by-step process of getting a project ready for printing proceeds from rough sketches to a master or mechanical boards.

Whether a project is to be printed electronically or by offset, the printer requires *camera-ready* artwork. There are three stages in the process of getting a publication camera-ready:

1. *Thumbnails, comprehensive treatments (comps)*

Graphic designers usually develop initial concepts for projects in the form of *thumbnails*. These are mini-sketches of how a publication will look, showing the number of pages, folds, style of type and headlines, and use of color and graphics. These thumbnails are presented to the client early in the project.

Comps (comprehensive treatments) are mockups that are termed *loose* or *tight* according to how closely they convey what the final product will look like. A loose comp might use non-reading dummy type (also called *greeking*) to show how the copy lays out, and show sketchy indications of color and photos. A very tight comp will have all type and photos in place, in the correct colors, so as to be nearly indistinguishable from the final printed piece.

Most projects go through several stages of comps and revisions. The printer estimates costs based on the comps.

Thumbnails

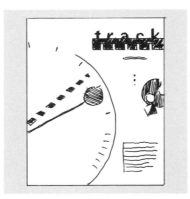

Loose comp

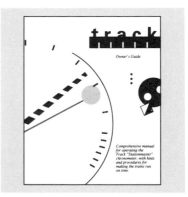

Tight comp

2. *High-resolution imagesetting and/or typesetting*

Whether or not this step is necessary is discussed on page 114. High-resolution imagesetting is done on continuous rolls of special resin-coated photo paper. The pages have to be cut and, usually, pasted on mechanical boards (see below) before they can be reproduced.

3. *Masters and mechanicals*

A page processed by a laser printer or imagesetter may be camera-ready if the job is very simple — one-color with all artwork incorporated in the computer file. This will often be the case with jobs to be reproduced on high-speed copiers. Such a page is a *master*.

The printer photographs the mechanicals to make printing plates. Any imperfection on the mechanical shows up in the printed product.

Most offset jobs require *mechanical boards,* usually called *mechanicals* or *boards*, sometimes *keylines* or *pasteups*. Made by pasting the typeset text and artwork to heavy illustration board, the mechanicals will be photographed by the printer. The mechanical must be clear and accurate, with precise guidelines showing page size and folds, with neat, unambiguous instructions for the printer. Everything on the mechanical — including spelling errors, misaligned artwork, smudges, and coffee stains — will show up in the printed product.

Line art, such as pen-and-ink drawings or computer-generated graphs and screens, is the easiest to reproduce.

Artwork and color require special treatment. *Line art* is the easiest kind of image to print. Examples of line art are pen-and-ink drawings, woodcuts, engravings, and etchings. Type, too, is line art. Line art that will print in one color is usually copied photostatically and pasted directly on the mechanical.

Multicolor printing requires separation of the artwork.

Since a printing press must put down ink one color at a time, type and line art that is to print in different colors must be *separated* so the printer can make a printing plate for each color. Instructions as to which items print in which color must be written on a tissue overlay (top photo, below) indicating *color breaks*. The printer will photograph the artwork several times, once for each color, each time masking out parts that do not print in that color.

If the color patches in line art will overlay one another, the person making the mechanical must pre-separate the art with overlays on clear acetate, as illustrated in the bottom photo.

Tissue overlays *give the printer all the instructions on color breaks, tints, images, etc.*

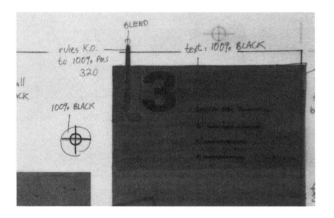

Acetate overlays *are required when images of different colors overlap. The printer can only make separate plates if the artwork is separated in layers.*

118

Pre-separating color work with page layout programs saves production steps.

Some desktop publishing layout programs allow the user to designate colors as part of the computer file so that separate reproduction-quality pages can be printed out for each color. Using the computer to pre-separate colors in this way eliminates some production tasks and reduces the potential for error.

Continuous-tone art is not pasted up on the mechanical. The printer will have to turn it into halftones.

Continuous-tone art is made up of an indefinite number of gradated tones. Examples of continuous-tone art are photographs, charcoal, pencil or wash drawings, watercolors, and oil paintings. "Black-and-white" continuous-tone art is made up of shades of gray; color continuous-tone art is made up of tints and shades of one or many colors.

Since it is not practical to equip a printing press with hundreds of shades of ink, commercial printing uses the *halftone* process to create tones that look continuous but are not.

As illustrated below, the continuous-tone image is photographed by the printer through a fine screen, called a *halftone screen*. Light reflected from the image creates a dot within each "hole" in the screen. The size of the dot at any particular point is proportionate to the amount of light coming through the screen; a dot may be a 5% dot, a 50% dot, a 100% dot, or no dot at all. A collection of printed 10% dots appear to the eye as a light gray.

A typical halftone has a resolution of 150 dots per inch. It is made with a 150-line screen.

Halftone screens are made by cementing together clear plates etched with straight lines. The screen ruling (the number of lines per inch) determines the number of dots per inch. Hence, halftone resolution is usually expressed as a line screen value.

150-line halftone

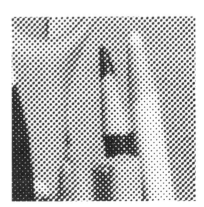

150-line halftone magnified

Halftones are classified in terms of their dot resolution. The more dots, the harder it is for the eye to resolve individual dots and the sharper the printed picture looks.

Making a halftone is simple and inexpensive ($15 is a typical charge). The key determinant of halftone quality is the quality of the original artwork.

Halftone screen resolutions

85-line halftone

100-line halftone

133-line halftone

150-line halftone

Special halftone screens create unusual effects.

Fine mezzotint

Coarse mezzotint

Straight line

Sunburst

Continuous-tone artwork can be resized by the printer.

Original continuous-tone artwork may be supplied to the printer in the form of *reflective copy* (prints) or *transparencies*. The mechanical artist indicates the size and location of the artwork on the mechanical with a photostat marked *FPO* (for position only), pasting down the artwork itself (except transparencies) on its own board(s) for shooting. The mechanical may indicate instructions for scaling the artwork (changing the size of the original without changing its dimensions) or cropping it (zooming in, cutting out parts).

Scaling artwork

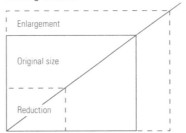

Cropping to use a portion of the artwork

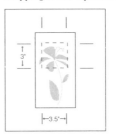

Halftone dot vs. laser spot

Professional-level computer software is available to turn scanned images into high-resolution halftones, obviating the need for some of the mechanical work described above. However, it is important to distinguish the photographic halftone dot from the dot produced by a computer. A photographic dot can be any size, filling from 0–100% of a cell in the halftone screen; a 150-line screen prints 150 of these variable dots to the inch. The centers of the dots are 1/150th of an inch apart.

The size of each dot determines the *gray scale*: the eye sees a 100% dot as black, a 50% dot as medium gray, a 10% dot as very light gray. Depending on the subtlety of the image, it takes from 16 to 256 different sizes of dot to reproduce continuous-tone art.

To approximate halftone dots, raster devices like laser printers use a process called *dithering*, combining printer *spots* (a spot being the smallest mark the printer can make) into clusters. The number of gray levels the printer can create depends on the number of spots in the cluster. For low-resolution (300 spots per inch) devices like office laser printers, this results in an important tradeoff between the image's gray scale and its resolution: if

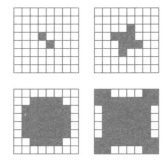

Dithered halftone image consists of clusters of printer spots, in this case, 8 x 8 arrays, each of which can produce 64 different gray values.

each cluster is made up of, say, a 4 x 4 array of printer spots, then each cluster can produce 16 gray levels, the minimum for acceptable halftone quality. But there will only be 75 of these clusters per linear inch (300 spots/linear inch ÷ 4 spots/cluster = 75 clusters/linear inch). This means that, on an office laser printer, the *resolution* of an image with 16 levels of gray is equivalent to that of a 75-line screen. However, on a high-resolution device, say, 2540 spots per inch, it is possible to get 256 (16 x 16) gray levels and the equivalent of better than a 150-line screen (2540 ÷ 16 = 159).

Computer scanning of original art and photographs is gaining acceptance in advertising and graphics studios, because the scanned image can be manipulated much more easily than a photograph and can be imaged by a commercial printer's color laser scanner. But for conventional printing jobs, conventional halftones are by far the easiest route.

Computer halftones are an alternative to photographic halftones, but not necessarily better or cheaper.

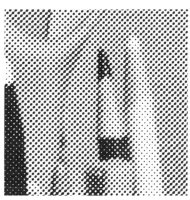

Halftone dot

Laser spot

Talking with the printer early and often pays off.

As is evident from the foregoing, the preparation of camera-ready artwork for printing can be rather exacting. No matter how the job is to be reproduced, it's wise to consult with the printer and find out exactly what is needed *before* starting the job. Planning the job carefully, and consulting with the printer often as to expectations, costs and schedules, reduces delay and keeps costs under control.

3.2 Electronic Printing

Electronic printing works by fusing magnetic dry ink to paper with heat and/or pressure. This technology is best suited to simple one-color printing jobs in standard sizes. But it is rapidly advancing toward full-color, high-quality reproduction.

High-speed electronic printers used by corporate reproduction departments and quick printers print up to 120 pages per minute. The image may be photocopied or created instantaneously on the printing drum from a computer file supplied by the customer. In either case, the actual *printing* is done by an electrostatic process, usually xerography. These processes are similar to those in desktop laser printers (described in §1.2).

Electronic printing is especially well suited to reproducing

- financial documents
- manuals
- proposals
- reports
- transparencies
- simple brochures, flyers
- legal briefs
- manuscripts
- address labels
- specifications
- price lists, sell sheets

Electronic printing is capable of producing quality equal to that of offset, with these important exceptions:

- Papers other than lightweight (20 or 24 lb) bond and xerographic paper do not run well in xerographic processes, particularly at high speeds.

- Color is expensive and difficult to control; this applies to colored type as well as colored artwork.

- Photography and intricate artwork do not reproduce well.

- Binding, cutting, and finishing options (such as die-cuts) are limited, because paper sizes are limited to 11-by-17 or smaller.

Technologies to overcome these limitations are developing fast. There is great affinity between digital computers, which work by recognizing on-off voltages, and processes like xerography, which create images by electrostatics (+ or −). There are some in the graphic arts industry who hold that these processes represent the future of printing.

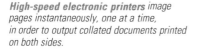

High-speed electronic printers image pages instantaneously, one at a time, in order to output collated documents printed on both sides.

3.3 Offset Lithography

Offset lithography — usually shortened to "offset" — is the dominant commercial printing process. Offset lithography can handle a wide range of printing jobs, from fine art reproductions to quick-printed flyers.

Jobs best suited to offset

Offset printing is the usual choice for quantities above 1,000 and for all color work. Following are typical offset jobs:

- letterheads
- business cards
- newsletters
- brochures and folders
- books
- postcards
- receipts

- envelopes
- flyers
- invoices
- self mailers
- carbonless forms
- announcements
- memo pads

How offset lithography works

Lithography works on the principle that oil and water do not mix.

Invented at the turn of the 19th century by the German Aloys Senefelder, lithography means "stone-writing." The lithographer draws with a special crayon on a highly polished stone. The stone is then washed with a solution of water, gum arabic, and acid. The greasy image area repels this mixture, but the rest of the surface holds it. The lithographer then inks the stone. Ink, a greasy substance itself, sticks to the greasy image area but shuns the parts of the stone where water adheres: *oil and water don't mix.*

The lithographer uses a powerful press to transfer the image from the stone to paper. Great art can be made by stone lithography, but not at great speed or in great quantities.

Lithographer at work.
Henri de Toulouse-Lautrec, Cover No. 1 of
L'Estampe Originale, 1893. Color lithograph,
17 ¾" x 23 ¾", Metropolitan Museum of Art,
New York, Rogers Fund, 1922.

In commercial lithography, image and non-image areas are created by photochemistry.

Commercial lithography replaces the stone with a flexible plate wrapped around a cylinder. It replaces the crayon drawing with a photo process: the plate is coated with chemicals whose physical properties are affected by light. Exposed to light through a negative of the image to be printed, the part of the plate that will carry the image becomes ink-receptive; the rest of the plate becomes water-receptive.

The "offset" in offset protects the printing plates and improves ink coverage.

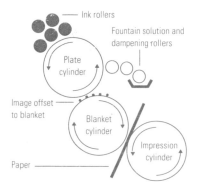

In offset printing, as in stone lithography, the plate is washed with a solution of water, gum arabic, and acid, called the *fountain solution*. The washed areas will repel ink, the greasy areas will attract ink.

The printing image thus formed is *offset* from the plate to a smooth rubber cylinder called the *blanket*. Offsetting eliminates contact between the surface of the plate and the (relatively) rough surface of the paper, extending printing plate life. The rubber blanket also conforms to the surface of textured papers better than could the metal plate, improving ink coverage.

A third cylinder, called the *impression* cylinder, presses the paper against the blanket for the final image transfer.

Commercial lithographic presses are of two types:

- *Sheetfed offset,* most commonly in sizes between 25" x 38" and 38" x 50", can print from one to six colors, at speeds up to 11,000 impressions per hour. Small sheetfed presses which run bond paper sizes are called *offset duplicators* or *multiliths*. Quick printers and central reproduction departments usually have several multiliths.

- *Web offset,* for printing long runs from huge rolls of paper.

Heidelberg GTO single-color press

Heidelberg Speedmaster six-color press

Multicolor printing

In the lithographic process described above, the plate transfers only one color of ink at a time. Each color on the finished job requires its own plate. Additional colors can be printed on a one-color press by changing the plate and the ink and running the paper through again. Multi-color presses (common types are 2-, 4-, 5-, and 6-color) have different plates at multiple printing stations (called *printers*).

To specify ink colors for multicolor type and line art, most graphic arts professionals use the PANTONE®* MATCHING SYSTEM. This system is based on nine PANTONE Basic Colors, plus PANTONE Black and PANTONE Transparent White. Mixed according to formulas, these colors produce hundreds of colors that match colors illustrated in *The PANTONE Library of Color*.

Spot color is used to accent type and line art and enrich halftones.

Match ink colors usually function as accents (*spot color*) in type-and-line work. Mechanicals must indicate which areas print which color. The printer will make a plate for each color and mix the ink accordingly.

Halftones, too, can benefit from an additional color. A common halftone effect is the *duotone*, where two halftone screens and two printing plates are made for a single photograph. The first (black) is exposed for contrast, to fill in the blacks, the second (color) is exposed for the middle tones. The result is a rich black-and-white-and-color halftone. An alternative is simply to print a flat tint of color behind the halftone.

Duotone

Flat tint behind the halftone

* Pantone, Inc.'s check-standard trademark for color reproduction and color reproduction materials.

Process color

Reproducing continuous-tone art with *all* the color of the original requires *color separation*, breaking down the original artwork into halftones representing its constituent colors, which will be reproduced using *process ink* — magenta, yellow, cyan, and black.

Here's how color separation works:

There are three basic colors of light — red, blue, and green — corresponding to receptors in the eye. Equal mixtures of these three colors produce white light; hence their name, *additive primaries*.

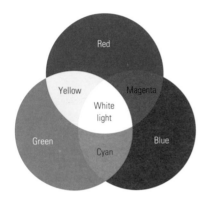

The possible combinations of two additive primaries are

- magenta (reflects red+blue)
- yellow (reflects red+green)
- cyan (reflects blue+green)

Since each of these combinations *absorbs* one color (magenta absorbs green, yellow absorbs blue, cyan absorbs red), these combinations of additive primaries are called *subtractive primaries*.

White paper reflects all colors

Yellow absorbs blue, reflects red and green

Cyan absorbs red, reflects green and blue

Magenta absorbs green, reflects red and blue

Black absorbs all colors

The color separation process makes a photographic or digital record of the distribution of magenta, yellow, cyan, and black in the original.

In the color separation process, light from the original artwork is passed through colored filters to produce information on its color constituents:

- With a red filter, a record is made of all the red light in the original. When a print is made from the *negative* of this information, it will correspond to the areas which did *not* reflect red. These areas correspond, then, to blue+green and can be printed with cyan ink.

- Similarly, a green filter is used to determine how much red+blue were in the original; this information is used to make the magenta printer.

- A blue filter contributes information on the distribution of red+green for the yellow printer.

In theory, the subtractive primaries should be able to produce all colors. In practice, black must be added for contrast. *Camera* separations were the norm until a few years ago — the separations were photographic negatives of pictures taken through the different color filters. Computer scanning, diagrammed below, stores the color information digitally. Computer scanning is displacing the older method.

Color Separation by Laser Scanner

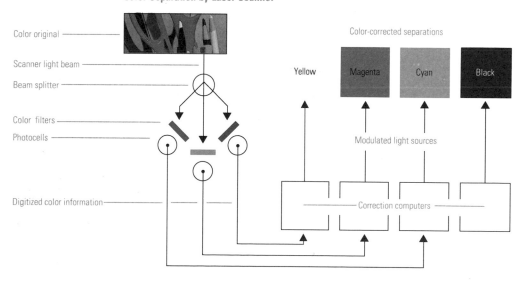

Color original

Scanner light beam

Beam splitter

Color filters

Photocells

Digitized color information

Yellow   Magenta   Cyan   Black

Color-corrected separations

Modulated light sources

Correction computers

Four-color process printing

Blue filter

Yellow printer

Yellow

Green filter

Magenta printer

Yellow and magenta

Red filter

Cyan printer

Yellow, magenta and cyan

Modified filter

Black printer

Yellow, magenta, cyan and black

From the separated images, the printer makes four halftone screens, one for each color. When the halftone screens of the subtractive colors are combined, the eye sees, not side-by-side dots, but the illusion of continuous-tone color.

Desktop publishing and color separation

Once the information has been digitized, it is possible not only to change colors, but also to add or remove effects and images. Moreover, using specialized software, desktop computers can interface with the commercial printer's color scanner. This capability is a considerable boon to professionals in advertising and other graphics-oriented businesses. Most desktop publishing layout programs can readily produce separations of line art and can manipulate scanned digital halftones.

Color proofing

There are a number of systems for producing color *proofs* from color separations which will closely match what will eventually be done by the printing press. Printing buyers will be asked to review these proofs. It is during this process that color separations, particularly those done with scanners, can be corrected or enhanced.

Printing

Film assembly and imposition

A good way to see how imposition works is to fold a sheet of paper according to the diagram.

After all printing images have been photographed, the negatives are assembled into *flats*, groupings of pages arranged to fit the press. Depending on the size of the press and the method of binding planned, there may be several ways to *impose* the pages on the flat, one of which will be most efficient for the equipment used. If there are only four or eight pages, the printer may print two or more finished units on each sheet. The imposition illustrated below is one of several that are possible for a 16-page job.

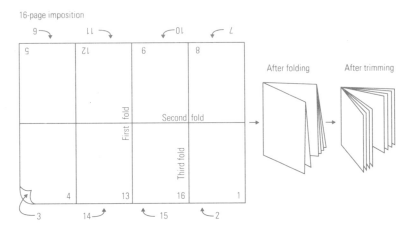

16-page imposition

Assembling films for platemaking is called *stripping*. In this process, skilled technicians (strippers) tape the film negatives in position on a sheet of plastic or colored paper, cutting windows to permit light to pass through the image areas for a particular printing plate according to the planned imposition. In process printing, a separate flat must be stripped for the cyan, magenta, yellow, and black printers. In many printing plants, automated cameras controlled by computers handle much of the stripping and imposition.

Blueprints: last chance to correct errors at reasonable cost

Blueprints (sometimes called *bluelines* or *blues*) are inexpensive pre-press proofs made by exposing special paper (both sides) to light through the stripped-up flats. In the blueprint, for the first time in the printing process, all the elements of the project come together — type, photographs, illustrations, and page sequence.

Although they are not perfect copies of the final output, bluelines should be painstakingly read to make certain that:

- the type is crisp and clear;
- there are no spots, specks, or smudges in non-image areas;
- no type or artwork has been left out in stripping;
- no pictures have been reversed, transposed, or left out;
- the pages are in the right order.

Correcting errors found on the blueprints (a spelling error, for example) is relatively inexpensive: it will take new type, a corrected mechanical, new film, a little stripping, and another proof to check. Once the blueprint is approved, however, corrections become quite expensive. At best, they require all of the above plus new plates; at worst, they may require reprinting the entire job.

Platemaking

Offset plates can be made using a number of different photo-chemistries. All work essentially the same way: light passing through the flats exposes the plate; the part of the plate that holds the image becomes ink-receptive, the rest becomes water-receptive.

Makeready and printing

Makeready is setting up the press for printing: fastening plates on cylinders, adding inks and fountain solutions, putting paper in the bin, adjusting registration, and fine tuning ink flow. Makeready for process color work can take several hours.

Once the press is up to speed, however, it will print several thousand impressions per hour. If paper is to pass through the press more than once, a few hours' drying time will separate the runs. Makeready for the second pass can take as long as makeready for the first.

Finishing and binding

There are many finishing operations. Most jobs are scored, folded and trimmed to size.

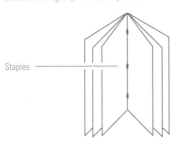

Saddle stitching is quick and inexpensive.

Staples

Perfect binding is used for thick publications.

Finishing is a generic term which includes:

- scoring
- folding
- trimming
- embossing

- die-cutting
- binding
- foil stamping
- laminating

Some operations may be done on-press, others as a separate operation after printing.

Many printing jobs require *scoring*, creasing the sheet with a steel rule, and *folding* it into 4-, 8-, 16-, or 32-page sections called *signatures*.

Folders like those illustrated at the right will then be *trimmed*. Other jobs will be *collated* (the signatures put in order) for binding and trimming.

The most common binding methods are the following:

- *saddle stitching:* the booklet and its cover are placed on a saddle (generally a steel chain) and run under a mechanical stitching head, which forces staples through the spine. This is the least expensive kind of binding.

- *side stitching:* used when there are too many pages for saddle stitching. The staple is forced through the side and the cover is glued on. Side-stitched books do not lie flat.

- *perfect binding:* used for bulkier publications, like annual reports and paperback books. There is usually printing on the spine. After collating, the backs of the signatures are ground off and a flexible adhesive is applied to hold pages and cover in place.

- *book (case) binding:* the signatures are sewn together and a cloth cover is glued on.

- *mechanical binding:* there are many varieties, including loose-leaf, spiral, and wire-o.

Finally, three sides of the publication are *trimmed* with a guillotine paper cutter.

*Some folders require no binding —
merely scoring, folding, and
trimming.*

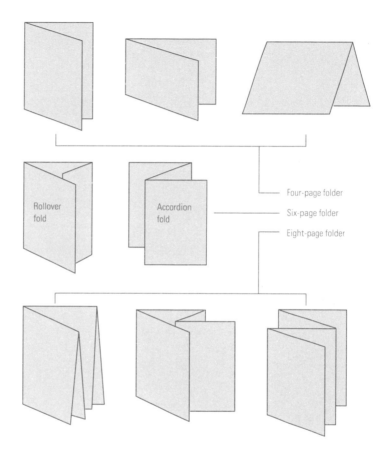

Rollover
fold

Accordion
fold

Four-page folder

Six-page folder

Eight-page folder

Packaging and shipping

All commercial printers do some packaging and shipping. Some
have *kitting* operations, where multi-item packages such as
computer manuals, software disks, reply cards, and flyers are
boxed and shrink-wrapped.

So that printers can include packaging and shipping in their
estimates, unusual shipping requirements, such as shipping to
multiple locations, should be discussed at the outset.

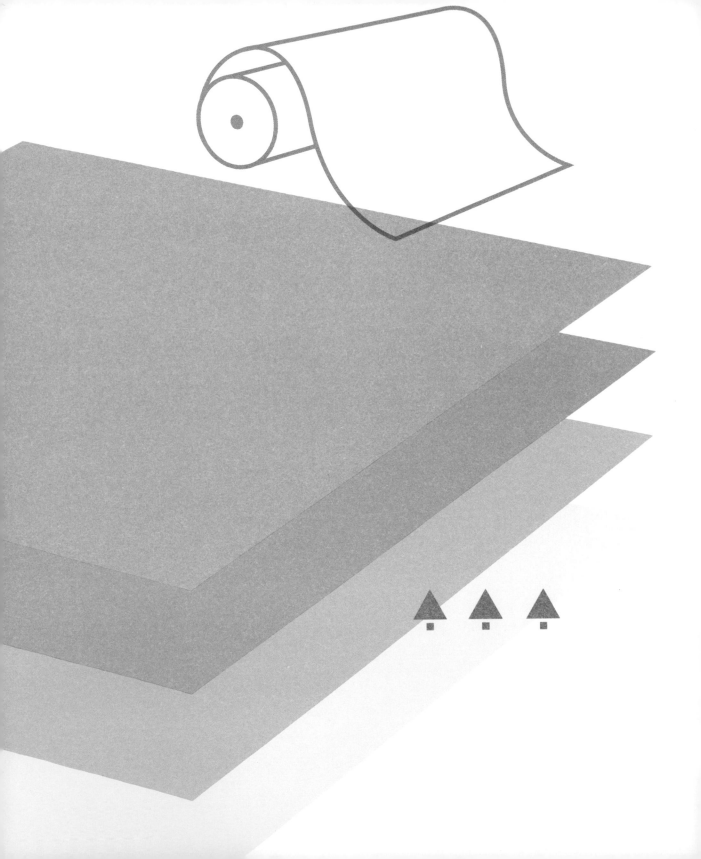

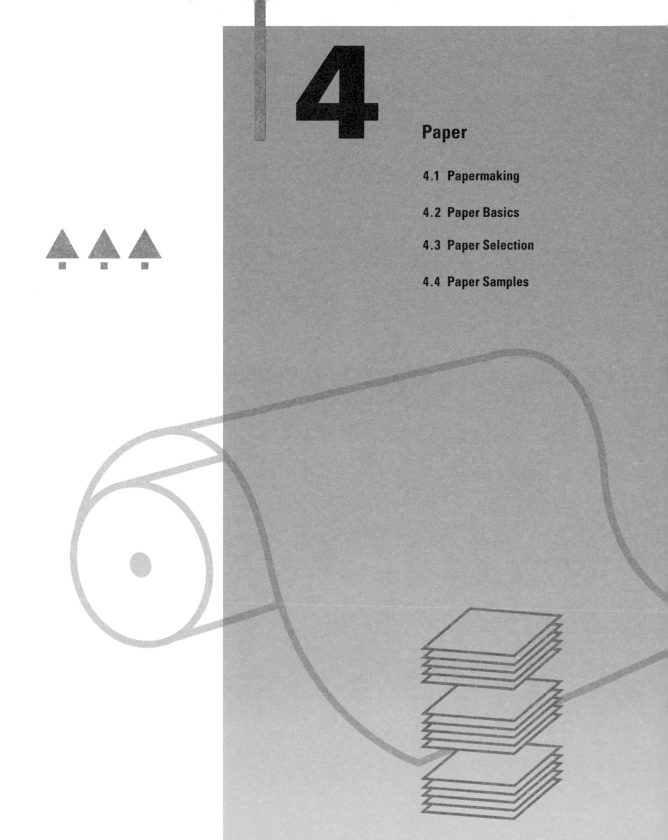

4

Paper

4.1 Papermaking

Developments in printing technology have been supported by advances in papermaking technology for centuries. Communication in the 20th century has benefited from great improvements in the quality and variety of papers for commercial printing, for office copying, and for laser printers and other electronic devices.

A very short history of paper

Paper was invented in China in 105 A.D. by the emperor's privy councilor and inspector of works, Ts'ai Lun. Up until then, the Chinese had been writing on silk (too expensive) and strips of bamboo (too heavy and hard). Ts'ai Lun made the first paper from bark, fish nets, hemp, and rags. He beat the materials to a pulp, then mixed them in a large vat full of water. He dipped a screen enclosed in a shallow frame into the pulp, removed it, and allowed the water to drain off through the screen. He was left with a soggy mat of fibers which held together and, when dry, became paper. The invention was very well received. Ts'ai Lun was promoted; paper came into general use.

Cutting branches

Boiling bark in lye

Washing bark

Making a sheet of paper

Applying sheet to drying board

Trimming sheets

In the 8th century, Arabs warring along China's western frontier captured some papermakers, with whose help they soon established mills at Samarkand, Damascus, and Baghdad, then the most brilliant and civilized city in the West. Under the Abbassid caliphs who ruled from Baghdad, Arab, Christian, Hindu, and Jewish scholars throughout the Moslem Empire used the new material to preserve the writings of the ancients and to transmit many new discoveries in astronomy and mathematics.

In the 12th century, the Arabs brought papermaking to Spain, and a little later to France and Italy. The flourishing commercial empires of Pisa, Florence, Genoa, and Venice provided an insatiable market for papermakers.

By Gutenberg's time (1450) there were paper mills throughout Europe. It is probable that, without the availability of paper, Gutenberg would not have invented printing. Printing, after all, is a manufacturing process whose essential raw materials are ink and paper. In any case, Gutenberg, who used superb papers which have lasted 500 years, certainly created a huge market for the papermakers: demand for paper has increased every year for 500 years and shows no sign of slowing.

The papermaking process

The process used in making 20th-century papers is the same in its essentials as that used by Ts'ai Lun in the 2nd century — removing the water from a very dilute slurry of vegetable fibers. But the paper industry has applied massive economies of scale and continuous innovation in process technology to keep paper one of the most cost-effective necessities of civilized life.

Industrial Papermaking

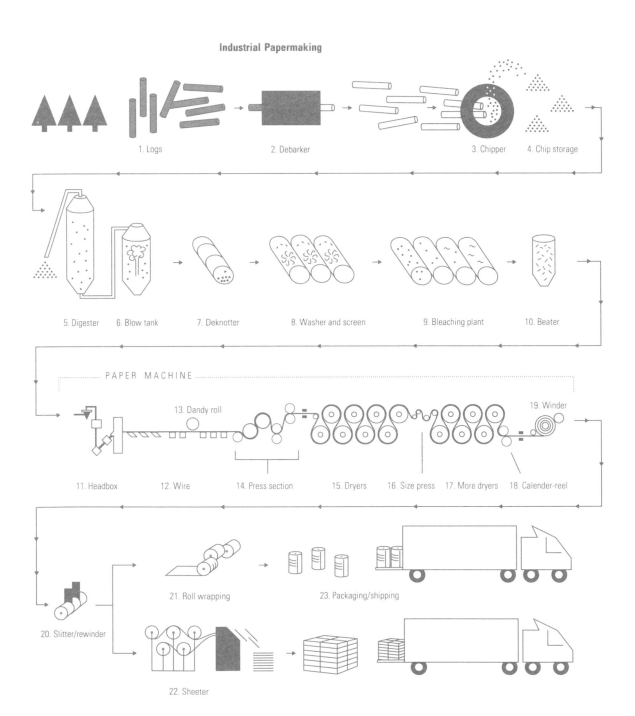

1. Logs
2. Debarker
3. Chipper
4. Chip storage

5. Digester
6. Blow tank
7. Deknotter
8. Washer and screen
9. Bleaching plant
10. Beater

PAPER MACHINE

13. Dandy roll
19. Winder

11. Headbox
12. Wire
14. Press section
15. Dryers
16. Size press
17. More dryers
18. Calender-reel

21. Roll wrapping
23. Packaging/shipping

20. Slitter/rewinder

22. Sheeter

Manufacturing printing papers

Chip storage

Digester

Industrial papermaking works this way:

Trees, cut into logs (1), are debarked in large rotating drums (2), then cut into chips (3), which are stored (4, photo A) and conveyed to the *digester* (5). Digesters are huge pressure cookers (photo B) which cook the chips in caustic chemicals under great pressure to dissolve the *lignin*, organic glue which binds wood cellulose fibers together. The resulting *pulp* is discharged to a *blow tank* (6), washed, and screened (7–8) to remove impurities.

Pulp for printing papers requires bleaching (9), after which comes *stock preparation* (10) — refining, diluting, and adding chemicals for strength and water resistance. The pulp slurry is metered at the paper machines (photo C) *headbox* (11), which sprays it onto a fast-moving *wire* (*fourdrinier*) (12). As the water drains through the wire, the fibers bind to form paper, which may get a watermark or special finish as it passes under a *dandy roll* (13). A *press section* (14) removes more water. Then the web passes over *dryers* and surface sizing is applied (15–17, photo D). The *calender-reel* (18), a set of steam-heated polished drums, irons the sheet to the required smoothness. The paper is wound onto a reel (19), which is slit, rewound (20) and, as required, sheeted and packed for shipping (21–23, photo E).

Paper machine

Size press

Packaging and shipping

4.2 Paper Basics

Paper quality is determined by

- printability, *the esthetic quality of the image as printed on the paper*

- runnability, *how the paper performs in the printing or copying process, throughput without downtime or loss of quality*

Each of the many grades of printing and office papers manufactured today has distinctive structural and esthetic properties.

Structural properties of paper

- *Basis weight (substance)*

Basis weight or *substance* is a paper's most fundamental property, a measurement of weight against surface area. Papers are often identified by their basis weights — standard copier paper may be called "20 pound" or "sub(stance) 20" bond. Most paper is priced and sold at so many dollars per ton, or per hundredweight or per pound. The basis weight of a paper stock is the weight in pounds of one ream (500 sheets) cut in the grade's *basic size*.

Each paper grade has its own traditional basic size. The basic size of bond paper, for example, is 17-by-22 (inches). A ream of 500 sheets of 20 lb bond paper in its basic size weighs 20 lbs. These reams will be cut into four 5-lb reams of the familiar 8½-by-11 20 lb bond paper used in offices. A ream of 24 lb bond paper in its basic size weighs 24 lbs.

24 lb bond paper has the same density and thickness as 60 lb offset. The difference is in the basic sizes in which their basis weights are measured.

Basic size: 17" x 22"
500 sheets

Basic size: 25" x 38"
500 sheets

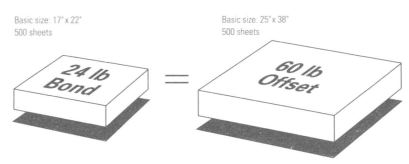

Papers shown as equivalent in this table will have approximately the same density. Other characteristics, such as finish, printability and brightness, may vary widely. Coated bristols are classified by thickness in points of caliper.

Equivalent Paper Basis Weights

Text Weight Papers		Cover Weight Papers					
Bond	Offset and Text	Cover	Coated 1 Side Bristol	Coated 2 Sides Bristol	Vellum Bristol	Index	Tag
Basic size		Basic size					
17" x 22"	25" x 38"	20" x 26"	20" x 26"	20" x 26"	22½" x 28½"	25½" x 30½"	24" x 36"
16 lb	40 lb						
	45 lb						
20 lb	50 lb						
24 lb	60 lb						
28 lb	70 lb						
32 lb	80 lb						
	100 lb				67 lb		
						90 lb	100 lb
		65 lb	8 pt		80 lb		
				8 pt		110 lb	125 lb
		80 lb	10 pt		100 lb		
			12 pt	10 pt			
						140 lb	150 lb
		100 lb		12 pt			
							175 lb
							200 lb

• Moisture content and curl

Paper readily absorbs moisture from the atmosphere; relative humidity affects printability.

Moisture content affects both printability and runnability. Cellulose fibers — paper's basic ingredient — attract and absorb water. If a sheet's moisture content is too high, it will go limp and cause printing distortion. If moisture content is too low, the paper will be brittle. It may curl excessively, crack when folded, and build up electrostatic charge, causing sticking and jamming.

Top-quality papers for xerographic reproduction and laser printing are manufactured with built-in *curl* designed to counteract curl induced by the heat in the printer. Excess curl is the most common paper problem, a cause of paper jams, poor print quality, clumsy handling, and binding problems.

Paper users can avoid curl problems by not leaving paper unwrapped on the shelf to absorb moisture: the ream wrappers of quality papers are an effective moisture barrier.

• Caliper and bulk

Caliper is the thickness of a sheet; bulk is the thickness of a number of sheets, measured in pages per inch.

The thickness of a single sheet of paper is its *caliper*. Measured in *mils* or *points* (thousandths of an inch, not typographer's points), caliper is a function of the paper's weight and *calendering* (pressing under steam-heated metal drums, like ironing). In general, the higher the caliper, the stiffer the paper.

Bulk refers to the thickness of a stack of sheets or pages. Measured in pages per inch, bulking thickness is a concern to bookbinders: the pages have to fit the binding.

Heavier-weight papers can withstand more abuse.

• *Strength*

Strength is the measure of paper's ability to stand up to handling. *Tensile strength* is the force required to break an inch-wide strip of paper. Tensile strength is important to printing papers, which are stretched and battered by the printing press. *Tear, burst,* and *fold* tests evaluate other aspects of strength. Paper's strength derives from chemical bonds between cellulose fibers; consequently, the higher the basis weight, the more fiber, the stronger the paper. Twenty pound bond paper is adequate for draft documents, but the durability and heft of a 24 lb (or heavier) sheet make it preferable for documents that will be read or referred to repeatedly.

• *Grain*

In manufacturing, coming off the paper machine, a paper's *grain* is in the direction of travel, but the paper may be sheeted to print either way. Paper tears and folds most easily in the grain direction. It also tends to *curl* along the grain. Nearly all office papers are *grain long*. Grain is an important consideration for the printer in folding and binding heavyweight stocks.

• *Fillers and sizing*

Fillers such as clay, titanium dioxide, or calcium carbonate are added to paper to improve opacity, brightness, formation, smoothness, and ink receptivity. Fillers account for 5–30% of a printing paper's weight.

Internal sizing resists water penetration; without it, paper is a blotter. *Surface* or *external sizing* is starch which acts as glue to increase surface integrity, smoothness, stiffness, scuff resistance, and folding endurance.

• *Paper defects*

Surface contamination of paper degrades printing.

Surface *integrity* is the soundness of the sheet: particles should not pick off during printing. Poor surface cleanliness results in voids or specks on the printed image.

The use of poor-quality paper in offset presses, laser printers, and copiers lowers production efficiency and may damage equipment. *Dust* can result from insufficient sizing or dull cutting blades used in sheeting. Evidence of dust includes specks or voids in otherwise solid print areas. Sometimes dust accumulates in the printer. In commercial printing, paper dust build-up can cause expensive downtime; in office printers, it degrades quality.

Other possible paper defects include folded or wrinkled sheets, holes, tears, and foreign material, such as glue from the ream wrapper, in or on the sheet. Paper that is too stiff or too limp causes paper handling problems in all kinds of presses and printers. It's easy to avoid these defects by specifying quality, name-brand papers.

• *Smoothness*

Smoothness is critical to ink holdout and toner adherence.

Factors in the papermaking process that affect sheet *smoothness* are the amount of filler, the degree of pressure applied to the sheet as it is dried, and the application of coatings.

Smoothness has a significant impact on image quality. In offset lithography, smoothness holds the ink up on the surface of the paper so that ink coverage is even and easily controlled. However, the lithographer can make adjustments to the viscosity of inks, and to the press itself, in order to accommodate a wide range of paper stocks, including highly absorbent and deeply textured stocks. Electronic printers are less flexible. *Toner* (dry ink) will adhere most evenly to a very smooth sheet, yielding the best possible density: black blacks and crisp lines. With toothy, textured paper stocks, toner may rub or flake off. The flow of toner can be increased, but only at the risk of having type and other detail areas fill in, making the overall texture fuzzy (reducing image resolution). As smoothness decreases, so do resolution and light reflectance. This is not to say that textured papers cannot be used in laser printers, only that it may take some experimentation to find which sheets work best. Papers with *laser*, *bond*, or *writing* in their names are a good bet.

Paper smoothness affects printing resolution. These micrographs (26x magnification) contrast characters printed on a 300 dpi laser printer using smooth paper (top photo) and a relatively rough sheet (bottom). Toner coverage on the smooth sheet is much more positive, resulting in better edge definition of characters — which translates to easier reading.

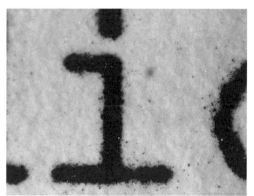

Smoothness also affects *ink holdout*, the ability of the paper to hold ink up on its surface. The better the ink holdout, the better the printed image will reflect light. Some papers — notably lower-quality offset papers and vellum bristol — "drink ink." Small type characters may fill in. Halftone dots spread.

- *Electrical properties*

Highly conductive paper results in image distortion and paper jams. Highly resistive paper causes static build-up between sheets, which results in misfeeds.

Visual properties of paper

Whiteness is color; brightness is reflectivity.

Opacity — lack of show-through — affects readability.

• *Whiteness and brightness*

Whiteness is a measure of the color of the sheet — which wavelengths of light are absorbed and which are reflected. *Shades* of white are the result of dyes or pigments added to make the paper absorb light of certain wavelengths. Blue-white shades *look* brighter than cream-white and green-white and are preferable for color printing.

Papermakers define *brightness* by the percentage of light (of a standard wavelength) the paper reflects. Most white papers measure 60–90% on this scale. Brightness is achieved by bleaching and adding chemicals; the higher the brightness, the higher the manufacturing cost: therefore, price is a good indicator of brightness.

When a printed image demands high contrast or brilliance, particularly in four-color process printing, the paper it's printed on should be very bright. Long text, on the other hand, calls for lower brightness paper, because reduced contrast makes for easier reading.

• *Opacity*

Opacity is the extent to which the sheet keeps light from passing through. It is a function of the amount of fiber and filler in the sheet, and the degree to which the paper absorbs ink. *Show-through* — the inverse of opacity — reduces contrast and detracts from readability and overall print quality. The average opacity of printing and writing papers is 90%.

• *Gloss*

Gloss is the shine that comes from clay coating added to the paper's surface, and from calendering. Although gloss is related to smoothness, smoothness is physical, gloss is optical. Higher gloss increases the printed image's brilliance and intensity. Most reading papers have lower gloss to prevent eyestrain.

Uncoated papers can be made quite smooth and glossy.

• *Coated and uncoated papers*

A typical sheet of glossy *coated* paper in a magazine or annual report is about 50% clay. Coated papers are made with either *matte* (dull) and *gloss* finishes. The matte finish papers have very high brightness and give excellent color reproduction, but they are less shiny. Coated papers are not generally suitable for desktop publishing because they are apt to contaminate the printer by blistering or flaking off particles. The papers used in desktop publishing are *uncoated*.

Uncoated papers can still be quite smooth and glossy — this book is printed on uncoated paper, Hammermill *Offset Opaque, Lustre Finish.* Generally, the smoother and more opaque the uncoated sheet is, the higher the contrast between the printed image and the paper, and the sharper the image. Very fine type prints best on a very smooth sheet.

But uncoated papers can have many different finishes. Paper-makers use embossing rolls, dandy rolls, felts, calender stacks, and other equipment to create such distinctive finishes as *wove, laid, vellum, linen,* and *watermarked.*

Watermarks *are non-functional trademarks applied during the papermaking process and used to identify high-quality papers suitable for letterheads.*

Permanence and pH

One measure of the *permanence* of a paper is brightness loss over time. Another is how the paper retains its strength. The higher the acidity of the paper, the sooner it will oxidize, and the shorter its life will be. For a permanence of 50 to 100 years, paper should have pH *above* 5.5; the pH of standard (acid) book paper is 4–5.

Alkaline paper lasts longer than ordinary paper. By 1991, all Hammermill papers will be manufactured by the alkaline process.

A significant trend in papermaking in the United States is the move from *acid* to *alkaline* paper. The alkaline papermaking process replaces titanium dioxide, natural clay, and to some extent wood fiber, with specially manufactured calcium carbonate fillers.

An alkaline sheet is esthetically and functionally indistinguishable from an acid sheet manufactured to the same performance specifications. There are two important differences: alkaline papers can be made whiter and brighter, and alkaline paper's pH of 7–8 represents a much higher permanence (up to 200 years) than that of acid paper.

Although only 25% of fine papers in the U.S. today are manufactured by the alkaline process (65% in Europe), economics, permanence, and increased ability to manufacture specialty papers favor the alkaline process. All Hammermill mills will be making alkaline papers by 1991.

Toner adherence

Toner adherence, critical in laser printing quality, is a function of a paper's curl, moisture control, and electrical properties (conductivity and resistivity). Laser printers and xerographic copiers use electrical charge transfer. If moisture is too high, charge is dissipated, and toner does not transfer to paper evenly, resulting in voids.

High temperatures (350-400°F) in high-speed laser printers and copiers like the Xerox 9000 Series can induce curl. Most slow-speed laser printers use a print engine whose internal temperatures only reach about 150° F, not high enough to be a serious problem for paper. On the other hand, the paper does have a comparatively long dwell time in contact with the printing drum, so there is still some tendency to curl. Heavier basis weight papers curl less. Slow-speed lasers also have a short paper path, so they can run a greater variety of papers than high-speed printers and copiers.

Many desktop publishers run pre-printed papers (such as letterheads) through laser printers. Letterhead produced by *thermography* (raised printing which simulates engraving) can damage a printer or copier. If a letterhead or other pre-printed form is to be run through an electronic printer, it's a good idea to tell the letterhead printer to use *thermal-resistant inks* and to package the material immediately to protect against edge damage and moisture penetration or loss. If thermal-resistant inks are not used, ink may eventually come off on the drum or fuser roll of the laser printer. If the package (e.g., shrink wrap) is too tight, induced curl may be a problem later. If a high-volume job on letterhead is to go through a high-speed printer, it's a good idea to make a short trial run before committing the whole job.

4.3 Paper Selection

There are only two physical variables in most desktop publishing output: toner and paper. Today, nearly all the toner used is one color — black. But the variety of papers available is dazzling. To a large degree, paper determines perceived quality. The easiest way to energize a publication is to print it on high-quality paper.

Bond papers

Basic size (inches)	Basis weight (lbs)
17 x 22	16, 20, 24

Bond and copier papers are sold in what the paper industry calls *cut-sizes* — 8½-by-11, 8½-by-14, and 11-by-17.

• *Bond papers*

Bond papers are office papers manufactured for

- durability, to withstand frequent handling, folding, binding
- stiffness, to make them suitable for letterheads, reports, and other business documents
- internal and surface strength, required for pen and ink, typing, and erasing

Bond papers range in quality and price from utility copier papers to watermarked, all-cotton bonds used for letterheads. Most bond papers are available in colors, many in a variety of finishes. Hammermill Bond is a high brightness, watermarked sheet for desktop or high-speed printers/copiers.

Laser papers

Basic size (inches)	Basis weight (lbs)
17 x 22	20, 24, 32

• *Laser papers*

Papers made specifically for laser printers are extra bright and opaque for high contrast. The surface is unusually smooth, so the sheet takes and holds toner particles very evenly. This translates to higher resolution (see chart opposite and illustration on p. 149). Moisture content of laser papers meets critical specifications for optimum performance in laser printers.

Hammermill's *Laser Print* is designed for *premium publishing* — where the originals from the desktop laser printer will be distributed. It has very high brightness and opacity, and a smooth, polished surface. Laser Print is also excellent for proofing jobs that will ultimately be processed on a high-resolution imagesetter. It is available in 24 lb and 32 lb basis weights.

Laser papers offer an ultra-smooth printing surface and top-of-the-line whiteness and brightness.

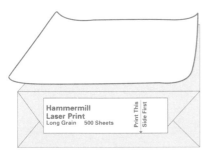

Ream labels on laser and xerographic papers tell which side should be printed first.

Laser papers print at higher resolution than bond papers.

Hammermill's *Laser Plus* is a cost-effective laser printer substitute for the resin-coated paper used in professional typesetting machines. It's designed for pasteups or masters to be photocopied or printed by offset lithography. One side of Laser Plus is ultra-smooth and bright for high contrast and resolution. The other side is treated with a wax holdout barrier, which prevents adhesives used in pasteups from bleeding through.

Some curl is built into all these papers to counteract paper's natural tendency to curl toward the side which is heated, the side in contact with the copier or laser printer drum. This is particularly critical when the paper is being used as a master in high-speed copying: a stack of curled originals may jam the in-feed mechanism. That's why it's important to know the paper path in a particular printer or copier: if the paper is placed in the paper tray according to the label instruction, heat generated in printing will counteract the built-in curl, so the printed sheet will come out flat and the paper will have less tendency to jam. It's also a good idea to keep paper wrapped, to retain moisture content.

Resolution and Printing Speed of Laser Papers

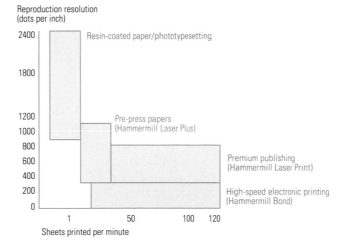

• *Xerographic (copier) papers*

Xerographic papers, smoother than bond papers, are designed for both low- and high-speed printers. Most are 20 lb; brightness is generally 80–85. Xerographic paper is useful for drafts.

Uncoated printing papers

Basic size (inches)	Basis weight (lbs)
25 x 38	40 (opaque only), 50, 60, 70, 80

Textured and colored papers make an effect.

- *Offset*

Uncoated offset papers come in a variety of finishes, colors, and basis weights. Brightness ranges from 75–90+. Many have matching cover-weight sheets. Offset papers absorb ink quickly. This is a benefit to the printer: the ink on the sheet dries fast, so presses can run faster. But if quality control on press falters, very fine type may fill in and halftone dots in photos may spread. The better the quality of the offset sheet, the better the ink holdout — that is, the less absorbent the paper.

- *Offset opaque*

Opaques have a higher opacity-to-weight ratio than offset papers. Lightweight opaques can substantially reduce mailing costs. Most opaques are very white and bright, with excellent printability. The brightness and opacity of offset opaque is well suited to desktop publishing with a laser printer, especially where there is heavy toner coverage. Offset opaque sheets are not recommended for high-speed xerographic runs.

- *Text and cover*

Text papers are heavyweight premium papers, available in a great variety of colors, basis weights, and textured finishes, such as linen, laid, cockle, and antique. Many are matched to heavier *cover* papers.

Text and cover papers impart weight and distinction. Tests of direct mail response conducted in the U.S. and in Europe found that mailings printed on textured and colored papers get significantly better results than the same mailing package printed on utility white papers (up to 92% better).* Important considerations in selecting text and cover papers are: Is the surface smooth enough to hold the edges of illustrations, diagrams, and letterforms? Does the color promote readability?

Where a job is to be printed by offset lithography from a laser-printed master, the "toothier" the finish, the better the paper will hide the fact that the type is 300 dpi laser type.

---

* Ian Dewar, "Paper's Role in Response," *Direct Marketing,* January 1988, 43 ff.; and an independent study sponsored by the Cover and Text Group of the American Paper Institute (1977–80), released by Direct Mail/Marketing Association, Release: 640.1, January 1981.

Laser printing directly on text and cover papers is chancy: the rougher the surface, the higher the chance that toner will transfer unevenly. Smooth finishes like wove are generally safer than textured finishes like laid, cockle, linen, and antique. However, the actual smoothness of these finishes varies from one manufacturer to another. The only way to be certain is to run a test. It's worth the trouble. Text papers are beautiful and distinctive papers.

Cover papers

	Basic size (inches)	Basis weight (lbs)
Cover	20 x 26	65, 80, 100
Vellum bristol	22½ x 28½	67, 80, 100
Index	25½ x 30½	90, 110, 140
Tag	24 x 36	100, 125, 150, 175, 200

• *Cover*

Cover papers — both coated and uncoated — are heavier-weight papers used for the covers of books and booklets, menus, cards, and so forth. Many covers are made to match the shade and finish of a text paper. Essential qualities are dimensional stability, durability, uniform printing surface, good scoring, folding, and embossing qualities. As a rule of thumb: cover stock of the same basis weight as text paper is about twice as thick.

• *Vellum bristol*

Vellum bristol is a durable utility stock. It is available in white and a few standard colors like ivory, tan, gray, canary, green, pink, and blue. Vellum bristol is less expensive and more widely available in cut sizes than are true cover papers. It is particularly popular with quick printers, because it absorbs ink quickly and dries fast. Caution: as with offset paper, the absorbency of vellum bristol may lead to murky halftone reproduction.

• *Index*

Index is a smooth, durable, heavyweight stock suitable for section dividers or covers. It is available in white and a few standard index card colors like canary, green, blue, and cherry.

• *Tag*

Tag is very smooth, very stiff, highly durable, even somewhat water resistant. It is available in white, manila, and a few standard colors.

Coated papers

• *Commodity and premium coated papers*

Coated papers are used primarily in commercial printing, not in offices (see p. 151). Coated printing papers are available in a variety of grades and qualities and are specifically engineered for standard printing processes such as sheetfed offset, web offset, and gravure.

The quality and price of coated papers can be inferred from the grade number. *Number One Offset Enamel* and *Number One Super-Premium* papers are the brightest and most expensive. *Coated Number Five* is standard in mass-circulation magazines and catalogs. The basic size is the same as uncoated offset, 25-by-38.

Colored papers

White papers reproduce halftone photographs more accurately and brilliantly than colored papers, since the brightest highlight in a printed halftone is the color of the paper.

Dozens of colors are available — they provide contrast to the black toner of laser printers.

But color adds distinction. Colored stocks are useful for

• proposal and brochure covers

• flyers and announcements

• letterheads

• newsletters

• mailings

The contrast between colored paper and black toner can be very effective.

Special-purpose papers

• *Thermal papers*

Thermal paper, like that used in fax machines, is chemically treated to turn brown or black where it is heated. Thermal *transfer* papers, used in some color printers, are ultra-smooth, bond-type papers made to adhere to heated wax.

• *Inkjet papers*

Inkjet printing requires quick absorbency combined with good ink holdout. Some inkjet printers require specially coated papers.

- *Specialty papers*

Paper is a very versatile substance which can be converted into many specialty items, such as duplex sheets, fluorescent tags, foils, and sheets embossed to feel like leather and other textures.

Specialty art papers and pre-printed colored papers can be purchased from graphic arts suppliers. As with colored papers, these specialties are particularly useful in adding interest and variety to publications printed on laser printers where the only image color is black.

Paper buying

Selecting a paper stock to energize a publication is a matter of examining what's available and deciding what's appropriate. In the case of very demanding color or specialty applications, the choice is critical. There is plenty of expert assistance available. Most printing paper distributors (paper merchants) make free samples available to their customers — chiefly printers, corporate reproduction departments, and stationers. Paper merchants may also employ *specifier* salespeople, who call on graphic designers and advertising agencies to keep them informed about new grades and applications. Thus, the best sources of paper information are

- paper merchants
- commercial printers
- corporate reproduction departments
- agency printing buyers
- graphic designers

There is no easier or more certain way to add quality than to print on quality paper.

Paper is not only an essential of desktop publishing, it is also a powerful ally capable of bringing weight and prestige to any publishing project. Desktop publishers should make themselves aware of the varieties of paper available and experiment to find what works for them. There is no easier or more certain way to add quality to a publication than to print it on quality paper.

The cost of paper is a function of brightness, weight, and appearance.

Paper *cost* is a function of quality — an indication of its brightness, weight, and appearance. The differences in the costs of various grades are indexed in the chart opposite.

For everyday copying and for printing drafts from a laser printer, any utility paper will do. Top-quality branded utility papers cost very little more than unbranded papers. Their advantage is that they jam less often and leave behind less paper dust and other foreign materials to foul the printer.

Standardizing for economy and quality

Not all the grades indexed in the chart are available in the small quantities and sizes appropriate for most desktop publishing. For simplicity and economy, it's a good idea to standardize on a few grades and colors *stocked* by a paper merchant, supplementing these choices with smaller quantities from stationers, office supply stores, and other specialty suppliers. A business may choose to maintain its own stock of standard papers, but should keep in mind that paper stored in a normal office environment longer than six months will deteriorate.

Index of Costs of Various Grades and Weights of Uncoated Papers

Indexed cost of paper required to produce 1,000 16-page, 8½-by-11 brochures (20 lb utility bond or copier paper = 100):

- *Price increases as depth of color increases.*

- *Price increases as basis weight increases.*

- *Connecting lines show the price of the same grade of paper at different basis weights.*

- *Numbers in parentheses indicate brightness.*

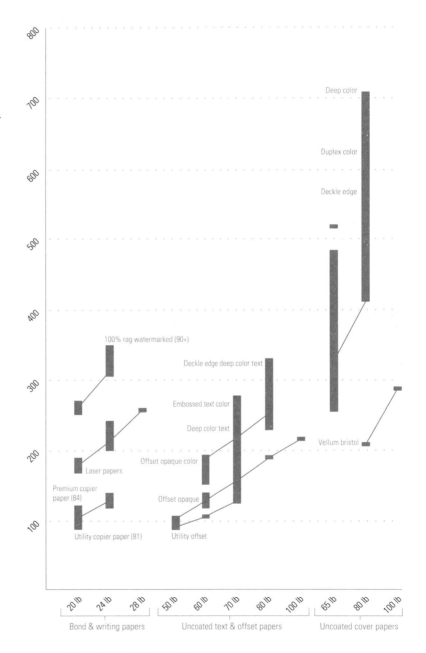

Source: Hammermill Papers estimates.

4.4 Paper Samples

The following pages are samples of Hammermill's Desktop Papers. These papers are specially formulated for laser printers, with a smooth surface that permits very even toner coverage. (Of course, the samples in this book are printed with black ink by offset lithography.)

Look and feel

In sampling paper, people rely on look and feel. In the paper samples which follow, we've shown some typical desktop publishing applications on Hammermill's line of Desktop Papers. It's worth looking at the fine print in evaluating printed samples — that's how to determine the paper's resolution. With rough papers, toner does not adhere well, degrading resolution.

The samples are by no means exhaustive: new colors and new laser papers are being developed and marketed all the time, by Hammermill and other manufacturers.

Vol. 7　　　Number 4

The Way to Communicate

Southwestern

January 1994

Newsletter

The Eightfold Way

Eiusmodi fabulae vibrabant, cum Trimalchio intravit et detersa fronte unguento manus laviteae spatioque minimo interpositomus.

Ignociste mihi inquit amici, multis iam diebus venter mihi non buami respondit. Nec medici se vamus ducuinveniunt. Profuit mihi tamen malicorium et taedade ex aceto. Spero tamen, iamae veterem feliisw Fepudorem sibi imponit. Alioquin circa deturamus stomachum mihi sonat, dis putes taurum. Itaque si quis quas quasin vestrum voluerit sua re causauali facere, non est quod illum iliumo pudeatur. Nemo nostrum solidem natus est. Ego nullum puto tam magnum tormentum esse quammi continere.

Hoc solum vetare ne Iovis ffare potest. Rides, Fortunata, quae soles me nocte dosomnemio fare facere? Nec tamen in triclinio ullum vetuo facere quod se iuvet, et medici vetant continere. Vel si quid plus venit, omnia foras de parata sunt: aqua, lasani et cetera minutalia. Credite mihi, anathum ymiasis in cerebrum it et in toto corpore fluctum facit. Multos scio

inveniunt. Profuit mihi tamenae malicorium et taeda ex aceto. Spe spero tamen, iam veterem.

An Accelerator Test

Profuit mihi tamen malicorium et taeda ex aceto. Spero tamen, iam veterem pudorem sibi imponit. Alioquin circa stomachum mihi sonat, putes taurum. Itaque si quis vestrum voluerit sua re causa facere, non est quod illum quasim pudeatur.

Nemo nostrum solide natus est. Ego nullum puto tam magnum tormentum esse quam continere. Hoc solum vetare ne Iovis potest. Rides, Fortunata, quae soles me nocte dosomnem facere? Nectur tamen in triclinio ullum vetuo facere quod se iuvet, et medicini vetant continere. Vel si quid plusu venit, omnia foras parata sunt: aqua, lasani et cetera minutalia. I Credite mihi, Eiusmodi fabulaem vibrabant, cum.

Trimalchio intravit et detersa sor fronte unguento manus lavitamus spatioque minimo interposito ignociste mihi inquit amici, mul iam diebus venter mihi non script respondit. Nec medici se.

"When ideas fail, words come in very handy"

—Faust

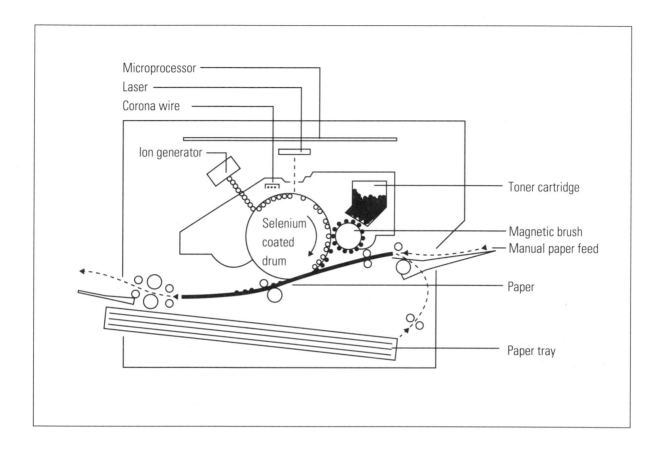

Microprocessor

Laser

Corona wire

Ion generator

Toner cartridge

Selenium coated drum

Magnetic brush

Manual paper feed

Paper

Paper tray

■ **Crosby Advertising**   320 Apex Road, Albany, NY 12201
a Division of Jarrow Pharmaceuticals

August 4, 1993

From:
Steve McFeirson

Management Report:

New Directors' Staff

Eiusmodi fabulae vibrabant, cum Trimalchio intravit et detersa fronte unguento manus lavit spatioque minimo interposito ignociste mihi inquit amici, multis iam diebus venter mihi non respondit.

To:

Lawrence Berkowitz

Janice Rosenthal

Jonathan Wovsepian

Denise Schweizer

Nec medici se inveniunt. Profuit mihi tamen malicorium et taeda exteriu aceto. Spero tamen, iam veterem pudorem sibi imponit. Alioquin circa stomachum mihi sonat, putes taurum. Itaque si quis vestrum voluerit sua re causa facere, non est quod illum pudeatur. Nemo nostrum solide natus est. Ego nullum puto tam magnum tormentum esse quam continere. Hoc solum vetare ne Iovis potest. Rides, Fortunata, quae soles me nocte turam dosomnem facere? Nec tamen in triclinio ullum vetuo facere quod se iuvet, et medici vetant continere. Vel si quid plus venit, omnia foras parata sunt: aqua, lasani et cetera minutalia.

Credite mihi, anathymiasis in cerebrum it et in toto corpore fluctum facit. Multos scio sic periise, dum nolunt sibi verum dicere. Gratias agimus liberalitati indulgentiaeque eius, et subinde castigamus crebris potiunculis risum. Alioquin circa stomachum mihi sonat, putes taurum. Itaque si quis vestrum voluerit sua re causa facere, non est quod illum pudeatur. Nemo nostrum solide natus est.

Ego nullum puto tam magnum tormentum esse quam continere. Hoc pura solum vetare ne Iovis potest. Rides, Fortunata, quae soles me nocteturm dosomnem facere? Nec tamen in triclinio ullum vetuo facere quod sety iuvet, et medici vetant continere. Vel sl quid plus venit, omnia forasium parata sunt: aqua, lasani et cetera minutalia. Credite mihi, anathymiasis in cerebrum it et in toto corpore fluctum facit. Multos scio sic periise, dum nolunt sibi verum dicere. Gratias agimus liberalitati indulgentiaeque eius, et subinde castigamus crebris potiunculis risum.

Steve McFeirson

Grand Printer Distribution Center

MEMO

● March 10, 1992

To all distributors:

Eiusmodi fabulae vibrabant, cum Trimalchio intravit et detersa fronte unguento manus lavit spatioque minimo interposito ignociste mihi inquit amici, multis iam diebus venter mihi non respondit. Nec medici se inveniunt. Profuit mihi tamen malicorium et taeda ex aceto. Spero tamen, iam veterem pudorem sibi imponit.

Alioquin circa stomachum mihi sonat, putes taurum. Itaque si quis vestrum voluerit sua re causa facere, non est quod illum pudeatur. Nemo nostrum solide natus est. Ego nullum puto tam magnum tormentum esse quam continere. Hoc solum vetare ne lovis potest. Rides, Fortunata, quae soles me nocte dosomnem facere? Nec tamen in triclinio ullum vetuo facere quod se iuvet, et medici vetant continere. Vel si quid plus venit, omnia foras parata sunt: aqua, lasani et cetera minutalia. Credite mihi, anathymiasis in cerebrum it et in toto corpore fluctum facit. Multos scio sic periise, dum nolunt sibi verum dicere. Gratias agimus liberalitati indulgentiaeque eius, et subinde castigamus crebris potiunculis risum.

Richard Williams
Director of Distribution

**A Handout
for a Meeting**

The Name of the Presentee
July 31, 1992

*Presented by the
Present Company*

Headline: 36 pt Univers 67

Subhead: (but reduced in size for this handout)

- Bullet point in 24 pt Univers 47
- Fewer than seven words per line!
- Sentence style: not all caps, not initial caps
- Ending punctuation not required

Four-Column Table

	Column Head	Column Head	Column Head	Column Head
Item A	200,000	300,000	400,000	500,000
Item B	100,000	200,000	300,000	400,000
Item C	200,000	400,000	100,000	300,000
Item D	1,340,000	2,567,000	2,345,000	4,300,000

A Graphic Overhead

Caption in
14 pt
Univers 47

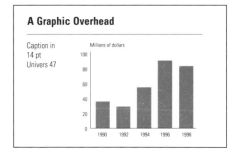

66 All things change, and you yourself are constantly wasting away. So, also, is the universe. **99**

— Marcus Aurelius, *Meditations IX*

Entropicana Inertial Systems, Inc.

New
From *The Manufacturing Concern*

Gizmo

A Revolutionary New Kind of Thing

Eiusmodi fabulae vibrabant, cum Trimalchio intravit et detersa fronte unguento manus lavit spatioque minimo interposito ignociste mihi inquit amici, multis iam diebus venter mihi non respondit. Nec medici se inveniunt.

Profuit mihi tamen malicorium et taeda ex aceto. Spero tamen, iam veterem pudorem sibi imponit. Alioquin circa stomachum mihi sonat, putes taurum. Itaque si quis vestrum voluerit sua re causa facere, non est quod illum pudeatur. Nemo nostrum solide natus est. Itaque si quis.

- ## Adrienne Eyre
  Rochester Institute of Technology

- ## Muhammed Al-Khowarizmi
  House of Wisdom

- ## John Kepler
  Elliptical Orbits, Inc.

- ## Sheryl Tui Tin
  Mancini & Company

- ## Takhiro Tanaka
  The Trading Company

- ## I. Augustus Stanwood
  Gardiner Mills

- ## Cicely D. Wrubel
  Foster and Faster

- ## Lili Yazmajian
  Consolidated, Inc.

Jefferson Buonarroti Goethals

Report and Recommendations

Jefferson, Buonarroti, and Goethals, Inc.

• **Restructuring**

Phase 3

April 30, 1993

Brass bed frame
Baseball cards
Beatlemania

Dry sink
Roll-top desk
Refrigerator-freezer

Men's,
Women's, ⎤— Wear
Kids'

Elvis memorabilia

More! More! More!

Multi-Family
Garage Sale

**Saturday
and Sunday
May 8/9
9 am – 4 pm**

**10488
Maplewood Lane
Fort Worth**

California Decks, Inc.

April 14, 1995

Bulletin

Price Hike for Boat Shoes

Eiusmodi fabulae vibrabant, cum laude Trimalchio intravit et detersa fronte unguento manus lavit spatioque minimo interposito igniciste mihi inquit amici, multis iam diebus venter mihi non folio respondit.

New Policy for Back Orders

Nec medici se inveniunt. Profuit mihi tamen malicorium et taeda ex aceto. Spero tamen, iam veterem pudorem sibi imponit. Alioquin circa stomachum mihi sonat, putes taurum. Itaque si quis vestrum voluerit sua re causa facere, non est quod illum pudeatur. Nemo nostrum solide natus est. Ego nullum puto tam magnum tormentum esse quam continere. Hoc solum vetare ne

Last Month's Drop in Sales

Iovis potest. Rides, Fortunata, quae soles me nocte dosomnem facere? O Nec tamen in triclinio ullum vetuono facere quod se iuvet, et medici vetant continere. Vel si quid plus venit, omnia foras parata sunt: aqua, lasani et celt cetera minutalia. Credite mihi, nautae anathymiasis in cerebrum it et in toto corpore fluctum facit. Multos scio sicu periise, dum nolunt sibi verum dicere. Gratias agimus liberalitati indulgentiaeque eius, et subinde castigamus bamu crebris potiunculis risum.

New Prices !

T-shirts	$21.00
shorts	$27.00
shoes	$54.00
jackets	$85.00

Consolidated Balance Sheet

■ The TransFinite Company

	December 31	
Assets	**1991**	**1990**
Current Assets		
Cash	$ 520,000	$ 380,000
Short-term investments	1,500,000	965,000
Accounts receivable	1,120,000	1,620,000
Prepaid expenses	150,000	85,000
Inventory	2,200,000	2,350,000
Other	85,000	25,000
Total current assets	5,575,000	5,425,000
Property, plant, and equipment	7,040,000	5,025,000
Other assets	500,000	250,000
Total assets	**$ 13,115,000**	**$ 10,700,000**
Liabilities and Stockholders' Equity		
Current Liabilities		
Accounts payable	$ 1,065,000	$ 1,625,000
Accrued expenses	165,000	225,000
Accrued taxes	85,000	125,000
Total current liabilities	1,315,000	1,975,000
Bonds (9% due in 2001)	1,500,000	950,000
Long-term loan	750,000	750,000
Total liabilities	**3,565,000**	**3,675,000**
Shareholders' Equity		
Common stock, par $1.00	7,000,000	5,300,000
Convertible preferred stock, par $1.00	350,000	275,000
Preferred stock (5%–par $50)	1,800,000	1,200,000
Retained earnings	400,000	250,000
Total shareholders' equity	**9,550,000**	**7,025,000**
Total liabilities and stockholders' equity	**$ 13,115,000**	**$ 10,700,000**

Q & A   Questions and Answers

Q. Lorem ipsum dolor sit amet, consectetuer adipiscing elit, sed diam nonummy nibh euismod tincidunt ut laoreet dolore magna aliquam erat volutpat. Ut wisi enim ad minim veniam, quis exercitation?

A. Duis autem vel eum iriure dolor in hendrerit in vulputate velit esse molestie consequat, vel illum dolore eu feugiat nulla facilisis at vero eros et accumsan et iusto odio dignissim qui blandit praesent luptatum zzril delenit augue duis dolore te feugait nulla facilisi.

Q. Nam liber tempor cum soluta nobis eleifend option congue nihil imperdiet doming id quod mazim placerat facer possim assum. Lorem ipsum dolor sit laoreet dolore magna aliquam erat volutpat?

A. Ut wisi enim ad minim veniam, quis nostrud exerci tation ullamcorper suscipit lobortis nisl ut aliquip ex ea commodo consequat. Duis autem vel eum iriure dolor in hendrerit in vulputate velit esse.

Q. Duis autem vel eum iriure dolor in hendrerit in vulputate velit esse molestie consequat?

A. Lorem ipsum dolor sit amet, consectetuer adipiscing elit, sed diam nonummy nibh euismod tincidunt ut laoreet dolore magna aliquam erat volutpat. Duis autem vel eum iriure dolor in hendrerit in vulputat.

Q. Lorem ipsum dolor sit amet, consectetuer adipiscing elit, sed diam nonummy nibh euismod tincidunt ut laoreet dolore magna aliquam erat volutpat. Ut wisi enim ad minim veniam, quis exerci tation?

A. Duis autem vel eum iriure dolor in hendrerit in vulputate velit esse molestie consequat, vel illum dolore eu feugiat nulla facilisis at vero eros et accumsan et iusto odio dignissim qui blandit praesent luptatum zzril delenit augue duis dolore te feugait nulla facilisi.

Q. Nam liber tempor cum soluta nobis eleifend option congue nihil imperdiet doming id quod mazim placerat facer possim assum. Lorem ipsum dolor sit laoreet dolore magna aliquam erat volutpat?

A. Ut wisi enim ad minim veniam, quis nostrud exerci tation ullamcorper suscipit lobortis nisl ut aliquip ex ea commodo consequat. Duis autem vel eum iriure dolor in hendrerit in vulputate velit esse.

Company Telephone Directory

Extension	Name	Department	Location
6333	Raffelson, Sally	Corporate Marketing	20th Floor
4557	Raines, Jack	Sales	22nd Floor
5695	Ramsey, Francis	Customer Service	25th Floor
7655	Reade, Maria	Manufacturing	30th Floor
8121	Reed, Ellen	Customer Service	31st Floor
7322	Reid, Fred	Planning	29th Floor
8736	Reade, Barry	Production Planning	29th Floor
5686	Riley, James	Organization Planning	32nd Floor
7644	Roberts, Samuel	Sales	20th Floor
5661	Robinson, James	Marketing	20th Floor
3769	Rodgers, William	Employee Relations	29th Floor
7117	Rodgers, Francis	Employee Relations	32nd Floor
5618	Rodriguez, Aida R.	Corporate Communications	30th Floor
6400	Rogers, George	Controller's Department	28th Floor
6734	Ros, Susan	Budgets & Controls	28th Floor
5829	Rourke, James	Employee Relations	32nd Floor
8333	Rowlands, Frank J.	Corporate Marketing	20th Floor
3387	Rubin, John	Sales	22nd Floor
8395	Ruggiero, Pamela	Customer Service	25th Floor
9934	Russell, Wilma	Planning	29th Floor
6231	Russo, Carolyn	Customer Service	31st Floor
6732	Rutherford, Alice	Manufacturing	30th Floor

The *Kwik* Copier

20 East Main Street
24 hours a day
7 days a week

555-1276

Pick-up and delivery available

Customer name _____   Telephone _____

Address _____

Black & White Copies

No. of originals	Description	No. of copies	Price
_____	_____	_____	_____
_____	_____	_____	_____
_____	_____	_____	_____
_____	_____	_____	_____

Back-to-back ☐   Collate ☐   Staple ☐   Special paper ☐

Binding

No. of bindings	Description of binding	Price
_____	_____	_____
_____	_____	_____

Special instructions

Subtotal _____

Sales tax _____

Total _____

Hammermill Bond, 20 lb, Pink

Richard A. Wilson   245 East 84th Street   (212) 555-3009
New York, NY 10064

Professional Experience

Bond Management Co., Inc.
1984 through present

Senior Portfolio Manager with responsibility for 33 accounts totalling over
$10 billion. Created 12 new portfolio funds for the Fixed Income Group. Managed
account relationships, including quarterly managment reviews. Developed a series
of new business presentations, which are now in use throughout the company.
Account responsibilities include:

Fixed Income Accounts
- Twenty accounts totalling $6 billion.
- Maturities of from 1 to 30 years.
- Sectors include U.S. Governments, corporates, mortgages and derivative securities.

Intermediate Fixed Income
- Six accounts totalling $2 billion.
- Maturities of from one to five years.
- Sectors include U.S. Governments, corporates, derivative securities and various short-term securities, including Eurodollar certificates of deposit and Yankee bankers' acceptances.

Cash Management
- Four accounts totalling $1 billion.
- Maturities of from one day to one year.
- Sectors include commercial paper and U.S. Governments.

Municipal
- Three accounts totalling $1 billion.
- Maturities of from 1 year to 20 years.
- Sectors include general obligation and revenue bonds.

Acme Pension Funds
1967 through 1983

Senior Investment Analyst

- Developed benchmark portfolios.
- Developed investment guidelines for fixed income managers.
- Designed and managed investment programs.
- Created and managed dedicated bond portfolios.
- Prepared and presented quarterly reviews to the board of directors.

Education

1964 through 1967

Cheshire University, College of Business Administration
Bachelor of Science Degree in Finance

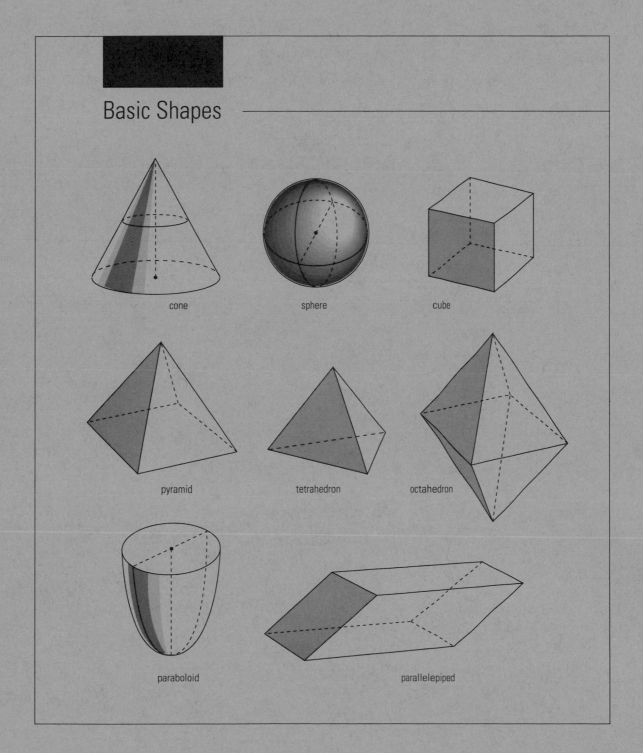

Basic Shapes

cone

sphere

cube

pyramid

tetrahedron

octahedron

paraboloid

parallelepiped

The *Kwik* Copier

555-1276   Fax Number   555-9157

20 East Main Street

24 hours a day—7 days a week

Price list

Effective: February 1, 1990

Black & White Copies

From one 8 ½" x 11" feedable original:

First 100 copies	$.05 each
Next 200 copies	$.03 each
Additional copies	$.02 each
10 copies	$.50
25 copies	$1.25
50 copies	$2.50
100 copies	$5.00
150 copies	$6.50
300 copies	$11.00
500 copies	$15.00

Color Copies

Color laser printing
From flat art:

8 ½" x 11"	$2.50 each
8 ½" x 11"	$3.50 each
11" x 17"	$4.00 each

From slides:

8 ½" x 11"	$3.50 each
11" X 17"	$5.50 each

Digital color copying

Self service	$2.00 each

Business Cards

500 cards	$20

Offset Printing

$50 minimum

From one 8 ½" x 11" original:

1,000 copies	$30
Additional 1,000s	$25

From one 11" x 17" original:

1,000 copies	$60
Additional 1,000s	$45

Envelopes

500 standard	$35
1,000 standard	$60
500 specialty	$65
1,000 specialty	$110

Carbonless forms

500 2-part	$85
1,000 2-part	$160
500 3-part	$105
1,000 3-part	$180
500 4-part	$120
1,000 4-part	$205

Binding

Under 100 pages	$2.75 per book
Over 100 pages	$3.75 per book
Perfect binding ($35 minimum)	$3.50 per book

Fax

Send first page:

Domestic	$4.50*
International	$7.50*
Additional pages	$2.00* each

*plus cost of the phone call

Receiving:	$1.00 each

Pick-up and delivery available.

Company Cafeteria

Menu for February 1, 1990

Open Monday — Friday, 7 to 9 am
and 11:30 to 2:30 pm

Breakfast

2 eggs, any style	$1.25
Pancakes	1.00
Bagel	.35
Toast	.30
Muffin	.45

Lunch

• Soup

Split pea	$.70
Vegetable	.60
Beef noodle	.80

• Sandwiches

Turkey	2.50
Tuna	1.75
Ham	2.25
Cheese	2.20
Grilled cheese	2.50
Pizza	1.25

• Salads

Chef's salad	$2.25
Tuna salad platter	2.00
Mixed green salad	1.75
Fruit salad	.95
Cole slaw	.60

• Desserts

Pie	1.25
Cake	1.25
Fresh fruit	.50
Cookies	.75

• Beverages

Coffee	.45
Tea	.45
Milk	.50
Fruit juice	.65
Soft drinks	.60

············ **ANNOUNCEMENT!**

Bold!
Wild! Sensual!
...Impossible?

Lorem ipsum dolor sit amet, pars et consectetuer adipiscing elit, sedum diam nonummy nibh euismod tincidi.

ADJECTIVE dolore magna aliquam erat volutpat. Ut wisi enim ad minim veniam, quis nostrud exerci tation ullamcorper suscipit lobortis nisl ut aliquip ex ea **preposition** consequat. Duis autem vel eum iriure dolor in hendrerit in vulputate velit esse molestie consequat, vel illum dolore eu feugiat nulla facilisis **object of the preposition** et accumsan et iusto odio dignissim qui blandit praesent luptatum zzril delenit augue duis dolore te feugait nulla facilisi. Lorem ipsum dolor sit amet, consectetuer **CONJUNCTION** elit, sed diam nonummy nibh euismod tincidunt ut laoreet dolore magna aliquam erat volutpat. Ut wisi enim ad minim veniam, quis nostrud **ADVERB** tation ullamcorper suscipit lobortis nisl ut aliquip ex ea commodo consequat.

NOUN vel eum iriure dolor intreado hendrerit in vulputate velit esse mesa molestie consequat, vel illum dol feugiat nulla facilisis at vero eros et accumsan et iusto odio dignissima **SUBJUNCTIVE** praesent luptatum zzril delenit augue duis dolore teanui feugait nulla facilisi. **VERB** temporta cum soluta nobis eleifend option e congue nihil imperdiet doming idaeim quod mazim placerat facer possi assum. Lorem ipsum **object** amet, a tasectetuer adipiscing elit, sed diam nonummy nibh euismod tincidunt ut laoreet dolore magna aliquam eratum volutpat. Ut wisi.

Wowie

Zowie!!!

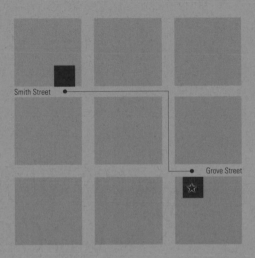

Smith Street

Grove Street

Kosmic Kamping Moving Sale!

Now through March 1st, over $350,000 in inventory will be on sale — thousands of selected items. Inventory from every department will be featured at 25 to 50% off — our way of telling you, our valued customer, that we appreciate your business!

After 32 years, we are closing our Smith Street branch store. We will continue to serve you from our new, expanded location in the Mountain Plaza Shopping Center on Grove Street. Come see us soon at our new location, opening April 1st.

Economic *Outlook*

Survey

February 19, 1994

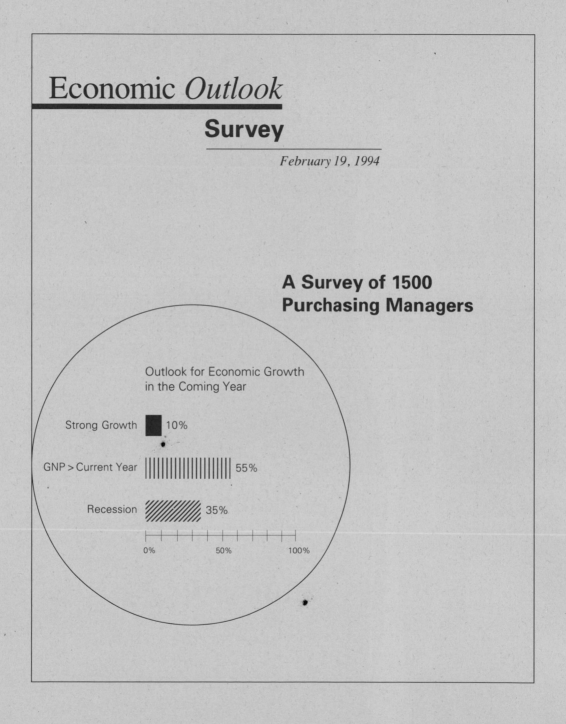

A Survey of 1500 Purchasing Managers

Outlook for Economic Growth
in the Coming Year

Strong Growth █ 10%

GNP > Current Year ||||||||||||||||| 55%

Recession ▨▨▨ 35%

0%   50%   100%

5

Desktop Presentations

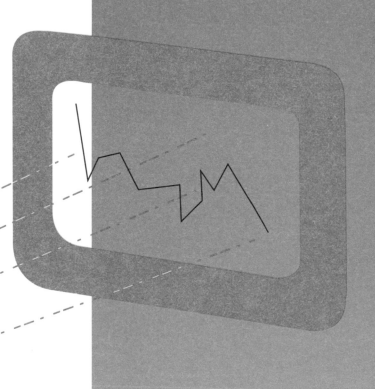
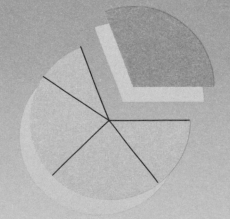

Desktop Presentations

According to a 1986 University of Minnesota study, more than eight million sales presentations are made in the U.S. every day. Add to this number millions of additional presentations, on topics such as research findings, investment recommendations, and reorganization plans, for example, using the same structures and media, and it is easy to understand why desktop presentations are a booming subset of desktop publishing.

This section offers guidelines for getting the most out of desktop computers for presentations in business meetings.

Audience and media

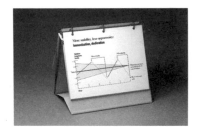

How the presenter and the audience will interact is the most important consideration in choosing a presentation medium.

- For a small audience, in an informal setting where give-and-take is expected, a flip chart, a computer screen, or overhead transparencies all work well. All can be edited or added to on-site; all keep the lights on.

- For audiences of 5–20-or-so people, overhead transparencies, a large computer monitor, or computer projection system are effective. Transparencies have the edge in informality and portability, but the computer can bring color and (for the present, anyway) novelty to the presentation.

- With large audiences, or where color photographs and graphics are paramount, the nod must go to 35 mm slides or big-screen computer/video. Capable of color, motion and sound, these media give the speaker the most authority and control over the presentation. But there is little interaction since, in most cases, the lights are low.

As far as preparing presentations using desktop computers is concerned, there are more similarities than differences among these media.

Organizing around visuals

The best way to organize a presentation is to begin with an outline. Computer programs specially designed for desktop presentations often incorporate outlining utilities. Outlines work by the one-idea-at-a-time, main-topic–subtopic logic that drives the most effective business presentations. Where several individuals or workgroups will contribute to the presentation, putting a computer outline file on a network, or otherwise circulating an outline for contributions and comments from responsible parties, can help resolve conflicts and reduce wasted effort.

Presenters use visuals to

- open the presentation, state its purpose, and tell what's in it for the listener

- emphasize key points

- present quantitative information

- make comparisons

- show relationships

- simplify complex processes

- explain new concepts

- show pictures

- state the conclusions the audience is expected to draw

In developing the outline or script, a very helpful practice is to describe each visual in terms of one of these purposes, stating the point to be made. For example: "Key point: rapid increase in productivity since Smith became sales manager" or "Organization chart [before I took over]: much duplication, many levels of management, muddled lines of authority."

Design and production

There are two basic types of visuals:

• *Illustrative visuals*

Tables, graphs, photographs, diagrams, animations — these are the pictures that are (or ought to be) worth a thousand words.

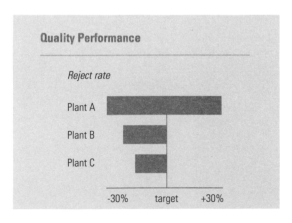

• *Word graphics*

Lists, brief tables, principal conclusions — using word graphics effectively, the speaker can help to determine what conclusions the audience will take away.

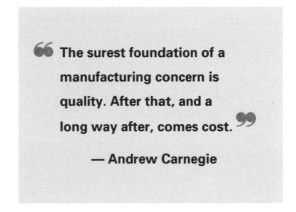

> **The surest foundation of a manufacturing concern is quality. After that, and a long way after, comes cost.**
>
> **— Andrew Carnegie**

If text visuals are to be the *only* visuals used by a speaker, it's reasonable to question the need for visuals at all. Unremarkable words projected on a screen are inevitably dull, may be distracting, and do little or nothing to further comprehension.

Topical bullet slide

Strategic Plan

• Goal: profit improvement
• Strategy
   – Buy low
   – Sell high
• Tactics
   – Reduce costs
   – Raise prices

Think big

All the presentation media used in business have this in common — they work best when they are attempting to put across one idea at a time: whether textual or illustrative, a visual should present one central idea. Some desktop presentation software even requires that every visual have a title.

Text slides (or screens) should have no more than seven lines, and no more than seven words per line. Type that is big and bold works best. Any visual needs no more than one font in three different sizes of type. For overhead transparencies, 18–24–36 pt is a good combination, with the maximum somewhere around 72 pt; 14 pt type is acceptable for tabular material. For 35 mm slides, 12–18–24 pt is a good combination, with the maximum about 36 pt; 9 pt type is acceptable for tabular material. For computer presentations, size depends on the size of the screen. To make type big and bold, sentences must be shortened to phrases, and phrases to single words. Graphics should also be big and bold, with big simple text labels.

Desktop presentation software

• *Slides and overheads*

Programs designed for desktop presentations contain powerful features for organizing presentations and creating visuals, both text and graphics, as well as speaker's notes and handouts. Some contain spelling checkers, outliners, spreadsheets, graphing, and tabling tools. Some include telecommunications modules for sending files to service bureaus for processing. Most can import graphics created with drawing applications or scanned images. All presentation programs provide formatting for on-screen presentations, 35 mm slides, and overheads.

Templates are a valuable feature of many desktop presentation programs.

Many desktop presentation programs provide *templates* for various media. These specify formatting options, such as type styles and sizes, alignment, types of bullets, borders, and color schemes. Templates are generally available for titles, illustration visuals, tables, verbal graphics (such as quotations), and topical slides. If they are not using templates supplied with software, presenters are well advised to create custom templates *before* writing the presentation: the format may dictate the length of sentences and phrases. Templates and visuals can be created with many types of desktop publishing software, but the dedicated presentation programs are most versatile and provide the most aid in organizing and reorganizing.

• *Animations*

Animation programs capable of output on the computer screen or on videotape offer many exciting possibilities for desktop presentations. Using these programs requires some technical know-how, some artistic skill, and patience. But the programs eliminate a good deal of the drudgery and repetitiveness of animation by interpolating the movements from a starting position to an ending position.

Like other graphics programs, animation programs can use images from a variety of sources. Special effects are often built into the program itself.

• *Interactive presentations*

Interactive media for sales presentations, dealer education, sales training, product demonstrations, and other presentations will be commonplace in a few years. Using large monitors, video cameras and recorders, color digitizers, and laser disk recorders, such presentations can be put together today using custom software and complex workstations, although the process is obviously neither simple nor inexpensive. Nonetheless, this is an area to watch: the power of presentations where the client or sales representative can call up specific video clips or respond to on-screen prompts by pressing buttons on a remote control device is undeniable.

Output

• *Computer screen*

Computer monitors and projection devices come in many forms and sizes. Desktop presentations with an active computer projecting on the screen require that the presenter be very comfortable with three things: the subject matter, the computer, and the software. Anyone trying to "fake it" runs the risk of having the meeting collapse.

• *Flip charts and presentation boards*

Pasting down a laser-printed page on a piece of illustration board, or putting it into a presentation book, is the easiest way to make an effective, professional-looking presentation that can be given anywhere at a moment's notice. Color can be added with markers, film, or foil. Color printers can produce page sizes appropriate for presentation boards.

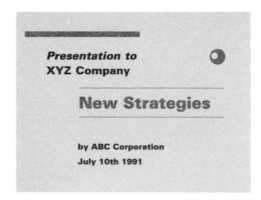

• *35 mm slides*

Desktop publishing systems can output 35 mm slides to film either by connecting a film recorder to the computer or network or by sending computer files on disk or by modem to a slide service. Turnaround is 1–3 days, and the cost per slide is low compared to traditional slidemaking services. Not all fonts and colors can be used. The most readable slides are produced by using the lightest possible color for type and other images and the darkest possible background color.

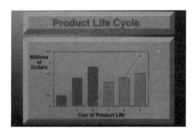
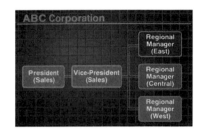

• *Overhead transparencies*

Overhead projector transparencies can be created on acetate with a laser printer, inkjet printer, wax thermal transfer printer, or copying machine. Since overhead projectors are usually used in lighted rooms and the projection is a shadow (dark image — clear acetate), colors tend to wash out; therefore, patterns are more useful than colors. Color overheads work best as reverses, like 35 mm slides — that is, the image in a light color and the non-image areas in black or a dark color. Transparencies of this kind can be made by hand (expensive and time-consuming) or, like 35 mm slides, sent to a service bureau.

• *Videotape and disk*

Getting computer files to videotape or disk requires hardware and software that convert computer output to standard video signals. An alternative to video is to store the presentation as computer files on compact disks using a special (and expensive) WORM (write once read many) drive. But the motion of the animation is slow, because the storage of video information as computer files requires so much disk space.

Afterword: Eight Ways to Cost-Justify Desktop Publishing

by David Shay

Director of Quality and Productivity

KPMG Peat Marwick

Afterword

by David L. Shay, Director of Quality and Productivity,
KPMG Peat Marwick

Eight Ways to Cost-Justify
Desktop Publishing

As Director of Quality and Productivity in a service organization which is, by many measures, one of the world's largest,* I study the interrelationships of productivity, quality, efficiency, and effectiveness in white-collar knowledge functions. Today, close to 80% of all payroll dollars in the U.S. go to these functions. Paperwork is our most important product.

This is not a sign that we have become a service economy, but rather that the *jobs* needed to be done by human beings are increasingly the jobs of research, reporting, design, quality assurance, marketing, and planning. This is a long-term trend, as you can see in the chart below.

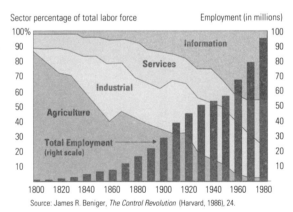

U.S. Employment 1800–1980

• Percentage by sector
• Total employment

Sector percentage of total labor force

Employment (in millions)

Source: James R. Beniger, *The Control Revolution* (Harvard, 1986), 24.

These changes are not limited to the U.S., of course. I recently visited a Hitachi heavy manufacturing plant the size of three football fields, chock-a-block with machines working to manufacture power turbines. In the entire plant I could find only nine operators tending machines. However, at CAD/CAM (computer-aided design/manufacturing) workstations in the engineering department, designing just the *piping* for the turbines, were *200* employees.

---

* KPMG Peat Marwick is the U.S. firm of Klynveld Peat Marwick Goerdeler, a worldwide management consulting, tax advisory, and auditing firm.

Desktop publishing improves the quality of publications, but desktop publishing on networks has the potential to improve the communication of knowledge among individuals and workgroups.

Clearly, in information-intensive environments, communication is critical. Even in the smallest companies, every white collar department is a customer of, or a supplier to, some other white collar department. Small gains (or losses) in each department add up very quickly. It is the promise of more effective communication that has driven the rapid growth of desktop publishing. The word *publishing* reminds us that the technology gives the user capabilities (but not, automatically, *skills*) that have heretofore been the province of printers, typesetters, and other professionals in the graphic arts industry.

Most knowledge workers, however, spend most of their time communicating ideas, not producing publications. In our studies we have paid particular attention to what might be termed *desktop communications*. We consistently find that desktop publishing systems initially purchased to produce newsletters or presentations become much more productive when made a part of a network. Networks of computers used for desktop publishing as well as other tasks have great potential for eliminating duplication of effort and making communication more efficient and effective.

Cost-justification

In our analyses of quality and productivity, we use eight basic types of cost-justification:

1. **Cost elimination or reduction.** The most sought-after cost-justification, because it is simple — fewer actual dollars are paid out for an ongoing activity.

2. **Cost avoidance.** Most companies today accept cost avoidance as equal to an actual cost reduction. Desktop publishing is frequently cost-justified on the basis of eliminating future expenditures, such as next year's typesetting expenses.

3. **Unit cost reduction.** When production of a particular item such as a report or proposal takes less time or costs less money, the unit cost has gone down. The originating department's annual expenditures may or may not do likewise — the money may be spent elsewhere, or more jobs may get done over the same period of time.

4. **Opportunity cost.** The value of opportunities such as increased transaction volumes achieved by clerical staff, higher quality products, new services for customers, or better planning.

5. **Reduction in elapsed time.** Faster production or delivery may bring a product or service to market faster, speed cash flow, or provide a competitive advantage.

6. **Quality.** The principle that the pursuit of quality increases productivity and reduces cost has been amply discussed and documented in recent years.

7. **Quality of work life.** Arguments for improving the quality of work life are based on the observable fact that happy employees are more productive; employees who are uninterested in their jobs cause errors, rework, and waste, and may drive customers away.

8. **Competitiveness.** The accounting community has difficulty placing numbers on competitiveness for cost-justification arguments. However, few executives will dispute the competitive advantage of higher quality or quicker response time.

I believe that managers should expect — and demand — results from their desktop publishing efforts which can be described under one or more of the headings enumerated above. Following are some success stories drawn from our studies.

1. Cost reduction

The easiest-to-identify savings result from the substitution of desktop publishing for traditional graphic arts activities.

The most popular way to cost-justify desktop publishing systems these days is with the saving of hard dollars paid to outside graphic arts suppliers such as typesetters, proofreaders, layout designers, and printers. The effect of desktop publishing on the time and cost of graphic arts production in a typical publication department is illustrated opposite.

Desktop Publishing versus Traditional Graphic Arts Production

Desktop publishing eliminates some of the steps (shown in the boxed area below) where it is easy to make mistakes and where revisions are expensive.

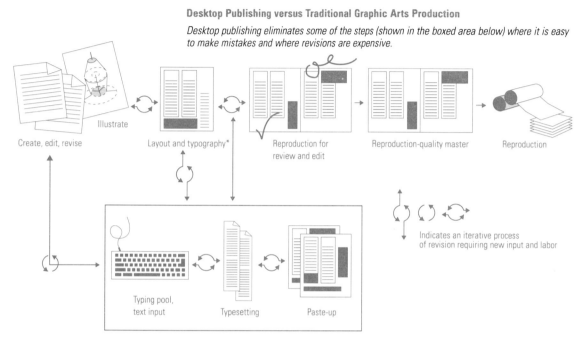

Illustrate

Create, edit, revise

Layout and typography*

Reproduction for review and edit

Reproduction-quality master

Reproduction

Indicates an iterative process of revision requiring new input and labor

Typing pool, text input

Typesetting

Paste-up

* Typography is the choice and arrangement of type. Desktop publishing differs from conventional typography in that type is chosen and set simultaneously, on the computer screen, and can be changed in an instant.

Eliminating outside support costs nearly always produces a one-year or better payback for the investment in the desktop publishing system. We have seen cases where large technical publication departments saved over $500,000 annually using desktop publishing systems; smaller departments may be able to cost-justify desktop publishing on the basis of a few hundred dollars saved here and there.

Desktop publishing on a network cuts in-house support costs and saves managerial time.

Operations that are networked achieve even faster paybacks. The graph below demonstrates the impact on the cost of routine meetings conducted by a telecommunications company to review progress on its numerous military and other government contracts.

Reduction of In-House Support Costs with Desktop Publishing

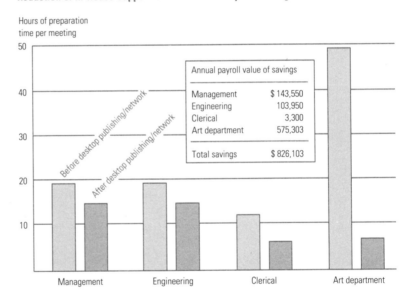

There may be many inputs to desktop publishing output — networks can eliminate duplication and enable specialists to concentrate more on their specialties.

The publications used in these meetings were overhead transparencies and handouts such as spreadsheets. The inputs to these publications included other spreadsheets, databases, memos, directives, reports, charts, and graphics prepared on computers connected to the network and made instantly available to the workgroup preparing for the meetings. You will note in this example that executive time is very much a part of the cost of preparing communications materials. To the extent that high-priced executive time is freed up for other activities, desktop publishing can contribute to a company's competitiveness. The cost savings here go beyond the salary impact: the art department is relieved of many tasks, such as re-typing visuals, which not only duplicates others' efforts but which also represents a highly inefficient use of graphic arts skills. One of the hidden advantages of desktop publishing is that it enables specialists to do more of what they specialize in.

Many companies, because of their size or the nature of their business, require in-house support staffs for art, layout, graphic design, or reproduction services. Not all such groups charge for their services, but there is a cost to the company. The supervisor of an in-house support staff usually keeps records of time spent for each job and can help estimate the costs that might be eliminated by desktop publishing.

The support services administrator may recommend that his or her organization own and operate the desktop publishing system rather than decentralize it. This is one of those make-or-buy decisions to which there is no pat answer.

Centralized desktop publishing versus in-department: professionals can do it faster. . .

On the one hand, typesetting and layout are far more difficult and time-consuming than word processing and typing. Other things being equal, professionals in the graphic arts can produce higher impact and more tasteful results faster than everyday office workers. As color systems come into use, this advantage will be even more obvious.

On the other hand, it's worth keeping in mind that

. . . but everyday office workers can accomplish a great deal with desktop publishing systems.

- using models or templates, everyday office workers can produce quality work with desktop publishing systems almost from the start;

- most desktop publishing systems involve a computer which can be used for other tasks;

- if a tool is handy, it will get used — people will develop their own skills and find new uses for the system;

- every department knows its own needs and business best.

Finding the most cost-effective combination of departmental, centralized, in-house services and outside services depends more on the allocation of skills than of hardware. Fortunately, desktop publishing makes it easy for people with diverse skills, including graphic arts skills, to work together effectively, especially if the system is networked.

2. Cost avoidance

One of the common uses of desktop publishing systems is to create fast, neat, attractive, easy-to-modify, easy-to-use, and inexpensive business forms. In one Dutch government ministry, creative secretaries equipped with desktop publishing systems gradually eliminated all but one of 40 official forms that had existed for years.

Business forms can be a lucrative source of cost savings.

The old forms had had many problems. Designed decades earlier, many were fold-over or multi-page forms, impossible to feed into today's word processors. Consequently, antiquated typewriters with wide carriages had to be kept on hand and in repair. The cost of ordering these official documents, many of low-volume usage, was very high. Changes in text by government officials frequently necessitated retyping entire forms.

Using their desktop publishing systems, the secretaries duplicated the official forms, preserving the image of the old forms as closely as possible, but redesigning all for standard paper sizes. Only one oversized fold-out form was retained, used by the Queen to memorialize special legislation.

Forms can be stored on diskettes, or on the network. They can be sent electronically for fast distribution, processing, and updating.

Computer versions of the "blank forms" were stored on diskettes and passed along to all secretaries. In this particular office, local area networks were used for communication throughout the offices, floors, and buildings. Once a form was completed in the originating office, it was sent electronically to the end-user department. If a last-minute adjustment was required, secretaries could update the form immediately, and it would be signed for processing. Before this system was put in place, changes to forms would be annotated, sent back to the originating department for retyping on a new form, and then returned for approval signatures.

Desktop publishing benefits in this instance are substantial:

- Thousands of guilders of actual cost reductions and repeatable cost avoidance were achieved.

- Access to forms at the desk cut turnaround times and sped approvals.

- Inventories of forms were eliminated. (Many companies find that up to half of all new forms ordered make their way into decentralized inventory locations — file cabinets and desk drawers — and never get used before the next revision of the form.)

- The new forms incorporated logos, graphics, variable type fonts, and other special effects which add character to the form and make it easier to use, edit, and read.

3. Unit cost reduction

Reducing the number of individuals who work on a given task reduces both unit cost and the potential for error and rework.

In most cases, *unit cost* reductions derive from reducing the number of people working on a project.

Unit Cost of a Technical Publication

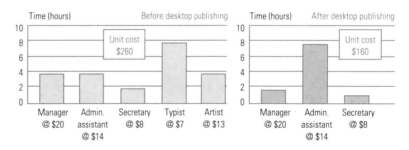

An easy-to-overlook benefit to this kind of cost reduction is that each person who works on a job takes time to get up to speed on the project as a whole, must schedule other duties around the project, and adds to the potential for error, schedule conflict, or missed deadlines. Eliminating or reducing these factors increases productivity.

Freeing up people for other tasks

Unit cost reduction is not the same as *total* cost reduction, nor does it necessarily result in the elimination of jobs such as those of the typist and the artist in the chart above: these individuals are free to do other, more productive work.

4. Capitalizing on opportunities

Most desktop publishing systems are driven by personal computers. Our studies consistently show that ease-of-use promotes use. We have found that specialized office machines dedicated to purposes such as word processing receive much less use than machines purchased for desktop publishing, which generally have easy-to-use graphical interfaces. Even personal computers purchased for the most popular PC functions — word processing, spreadsheets, and databases — get far less use.

Typical is the pattern shown below, taken from a study of a school district in the Denver, Colorado area. In this case many departments had purchased PCs for specialized low-volume applications such as keeping attendance records, class scheduling, and grade recording.

Use of Office Machines in a Colorado School District

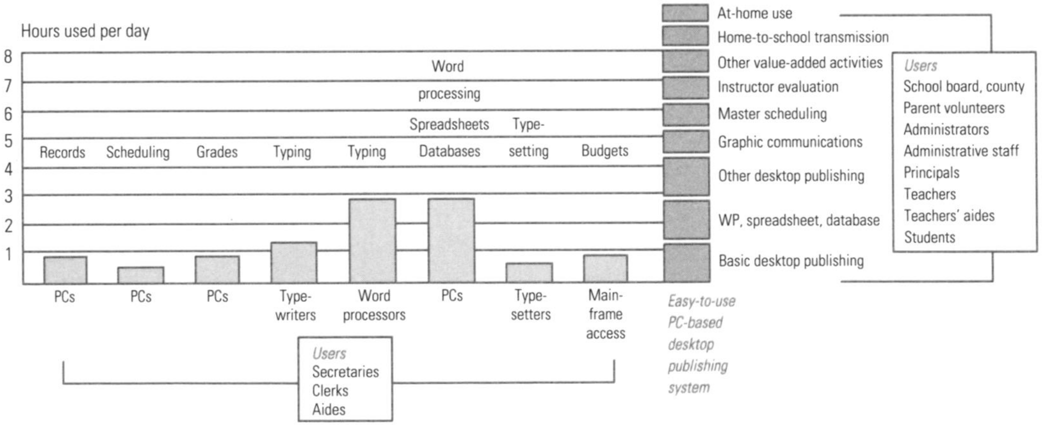

As noted earlier, most of the work in a society of knowledge workers deals with communicating ideas, not processing data. The chart shows that an easy-to-use system purchased for *personal* use often becomes a *workgroup* system.

Turning everyday reports and analyses to competitive advantage

A banker in Buenos Aires used a desktop publishing network to capitalize on a workgroup's effort this way: each morning, each of 11 executives responsible for tracking various market indicators updated historical charts and composed a brief commentary on his or her field. By 9 A.M. the annotated charts were in the corporate network, allowing bank professionals to call them up and/or print them out, for themselves or for their customers, throughout the day. Incidentally, as this bank was the only bank in the city to offer this service, the desktop publishing network not only leveraged the efforts of this workgroup, it represented a competitive advantage.

Usage rate affects ROI.

Assuming equal value to all the tasks performed, usage is a determinant of return on investment. If rate of return per hour is equal, then the more hours per day a machine is used, the faster it returns its cost. Under these assumptions, an easy-to-learn, easy-to-use desktop publishing system offers a significantly greater return on investment than specialized office equipment.

5. Reducing elapsed time

Helping to bring products and services to market on schedule

Almost every company must supply its customers and employees with manuals on "How to . . . " assemble, operate, maintain, understand, a product, service or policy. All "How to . . ." manuals have one thing in common: they are expected to be delivered with the product or service, which means they must be written, designed, printed, and in the distribution channel before the product or service is introduced.

A problem that often arises here is that if a change occurs in the design of the product or service — even so slight a change as the color of a button on the operator's control panel — *while the support material is in production*, how does the design change get reflected in the support material? With conventional graphic arts methods, incorporating design changes into the technical publications entails high rework cost. The alternative — shipping a product with instructions that don't apply — is equally unsatisfactory. We have seen instances where product launches had to be delayed because it took longer to modify operating manuals than to modify the product itself.

In contrast, we have studied a technical publications department which cut its production cycle from 15 to 3 weeks with a desktop publishing system.

Coordinating Design Changes with Changes in Technical Manuals

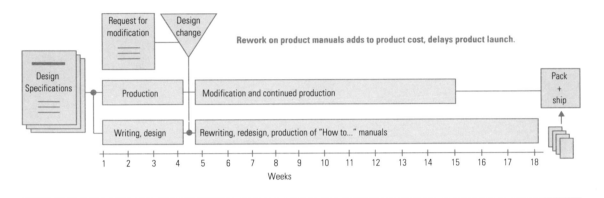

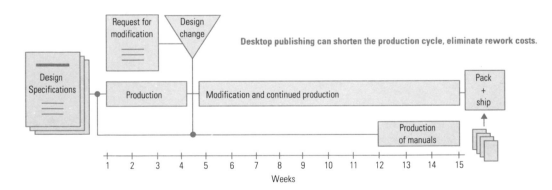

Assuming market acceptance, reducing time-to-market increases profits.

Reducing time-to-market can be a *major* source of profit: some pharmaceutical companies have used desktop publishing to get their patent applications through the Food and Drug Administration faster than competitors — by six months — thereby capturing market share and preempting competitive inroads.

6. Quality

Quality in desktop publishing affects the perceived value and importance of documents. When people think something is valuable and important, they pay attention.

In the largest Scandinavian utility company, higher perceived quality of interim planning documents cut the length of the planning cycle by one-third.

Quality in desktop publishing is not simply a matter of esthetics. A powerful example comes from one of the largest service firms in Scandinavia. The company is a utility which each year must publish a plan disclosing where and how it will invest its money in R&D, plant, equipment and resources, to keep up with shifting patterns of public demand. The creation and approval of this formal plan requires input from over 100 departments; it is ultimately reviewed by some 650 employees.

At the beginning of the process, each department prepared a draft plan, composed mainly of paragraphs, tables, and graphics cut with scissors from the previous year's typeset version of the plan, combined with typed or handwritten amendments to bring them up to date. These scraps were pasted up with new paragraphs and sentences typed on a variety of typewriters and word processing machines. It might take each department until the second or third draft to transform its ragged cut-and-paste version of last year's typeset report into a neat and newly typewritten draft of this year's report.

With the introduction of desktop publishing, this nine-month process shrank to the originally planned six months. Here's why:

Senior executives had not been paying attention to the first draft (and sometimes the second) because the documents *looked* like drafts. It was determined that close to three months of the planning process was wasted because those in the best position to know where departmental plans might conflict or fall short were too busy to get involved until the document attained the appearance and urgency of a final draft.

The new desktop publishing process begins with the distribution of diskettes containing last year's report; updates are made to clean files, and the printouts are clear. This eliminates the patched-together first draft. The first draft now looks like a *final* draft and immediately commands attention at all decision-making levels.

Upgrading quality of sales efforts

Another common use of desktop publishing is to create high-quality, special-purpose marketing materials. Frequently these are items intended for a few influential customers. Many would not have been produced at all by traditional means because of high unit cost.

Desktop publishing, combined with traditional graphic arts reproduction, can result in better targeted, more timely sales promotions.

We saw an example in one of Europe's largest consumer packaged goods marketers. One of the classic ways to promote these products is to provide retailers or distributors with high-quality, four-color glossy prints of the product, with "deals-of-the-month" described on the back. It was impossible to order long, economical print runs of the product photos because the deals were subject to frequent change, according to market conditions.

The solution:

- Order large quantities of glossies printed on one side only.

- Using desktop publishing, add type and graphics promoting special deals *as they are announced*.

The results were astounding! In pilot tests, the combination of high-quality color printing and high-quality, in-house desktop publishing produced the highest sales increases in the company's history. The approach has been expanded to cover many of the company's other products and promotions.

Desktop publishing, combined with database resources, can lead to more frequent, more focused, and more professional sales presentations.

The same computer system was used to produce graphics tracking each distributor's success in selling the deal items, and the associated profits. Each month a comprehensive set of sales graphics is generated automatically. Sales reps began using these graphics in monthly presentations to customers. The percentage of sales reps making such presentations increased from 5% to 90% in only two months. The professional image of the sales force improved, and sales showed a general increase.

As the cost of computer memory and processing power continues to come down, we will see new forms of desktop publishing. We saw one pioneering application in the corporate communications department of a Big-3 automaker in Detroit. They scanned 2-dimensional color product photographs into one of their most powerful 3-D engineering workstations. Using the 3-D imaging and calculation capabilities of the workstation, they produced dramatic images showing the product in — literally — a new perspective. These can be used for color slides, brochures, and handouts.

Reducing the cost of quality

Many companies find that 20–30% of total costs are associated with waste, scrap, rework, and warranty cost. Desktop publishing has been shown in many of these companies to improve the clarity of communication and to reduce rework.

One manager overseeing 42 engineers told us that, after giving his engineers access to graphic project management tools, he started to see graphs, charts, and tables popping up everywhere. These were the frequent topic of discussions between engineers and among project teams. He credited the higher level of communication with greatly improved on-time performance and greatly reduced rework, as charted below.

Performance on 1500 Engineering Projects

Effect of better project-management graphics in an engineering department

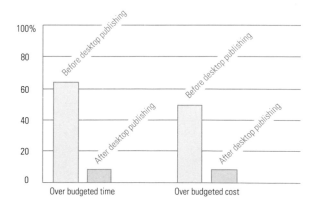

Quantifying the cost of quality can be eye-opening. Where poor communication is the cause, the discipline of developing high-quality graphics can produce startling results.

Management in another company felt that 20% of all costs were rework, and that close to 50% of all rework was caused by management's indifferent communication of goals, instructions, and specifications. When they recognized that this translated to $100 million in rework each year, they equipped their project managers with desktop publishing systems for developing graphics such as tables, line charts, storyboards, flow charts, task matrices, and other graphics to communicate their ideas. Because the stakes were so high, management *mandated* the completion of these graphical exhibits by project management teams *before* project work could begin.

Management judged that rework due to miscommunication was cut by two-thirds, representing tens of millions of dollars in on-time, within-budget, and profitable performance.

7. Quality of work life

Desktop publishing has several characteristics which improve the quality of work life:

- The tool is easy to use.

- It puts the user in command.

- It's usually fun.

- People take pride in what they produce.

The quotes below come from New Zealand, Australia, the United States, Canada, and Finland. We found in all these studies a renewed commitment by white collar workers to their work product. Where there is a sense of pride, there is better work.

Comments on the Impact of Desktop Publishing

"Whether I have a flair for the creative or not, or whether there are tight deadlines or not, the job is never rote anymore. There is almost always an aspect about the production that is unique to me, a personal touch that I enjoy adding to the product."

"I don't have to cut and paste scraps of paper that get lost, go to the copier and try many different reduction options, re-type articles in different pica to fit things on a page."

"People compliment and appreciate my work."

"I don't have to be held responsible for where everything is (at the typist, down in the art department, out at typesetting, etc.). I generally have everything at my workstation."

"See how the headings are in bold. Look at the shading, see the italics, the great graphics. See, we're having fish on Friday and I have a picture of a fish and a celery stalk. You should have seen last week's . . ."

With the better-looking output of desktop publishing, we invariably find that employees get complimented on their work. Whether it's a compliment from the vice president at the Christmas party for a great client presentation, or from a neighbor at a bridge party on the great new look of the school's newsletter to taxpayers, a compliment or "thank you" improves self-esteem and quality of work life. It's also a great motivator.

Here again, we see the amplifying power of networked systems. If you purchase a desktop publishing system for a graphic arts specialist that is difficult to learn and use, only the specialist gets accolades. If you purchase a system that is easy to learn and use, it becomes a workgroup system, and many employees enjoy the motivating experience of having their work complimented.

8. Competitiveness

Increasing advertising and customer loyalty

The marketing manager in a Texas branch office of a Fortune 50 supplier of film products recognized that many of her customers liked to advertise that they were using her company's products. The marketing manager saw an opportunity to save her customers money, increase advertising, and make sure her company's logo was prominently and properly displayed in customers' advertisements. The combination would amount to a significant advantage over her competitors.

She had already cost-justified a desktop publishing system to save on typesetting expenses and to create advertisements for her own company. She began supplying simple layouts to customers with copy — including her own ad copy and graphics — in place. This effort is credited with developing new customers, increasing the loyalty of existing customers, and increasing overall sales because of better, more consistent customer advertisements featuring the supplier's logo.

Rifleshot marketing pieces to customers and prospects.

Desktop publishing systems can produce very elegant mail merge letters, newsletters, or announcements. Customers may not take the time to read long fliers, product specification literature, or catalogs filled with hundreds of items they do not buy. But most customers will read a one-page memo on company letterhead addressed personally to them, especially if there is a dramatic chart or graph aimed specifically at them.

In a large New York City-based company, one salesman using such rifleshot marketing communications expanded a territory from $4 million to $10 million in just 18 months. Old customers came back, new customers signed on, and sales to existing customers increased across the board.

Summary

In summary, based on our worldwide research, managers are quite justified in demanding that their desktop publishing operations produce one or more of the following:

- cost elimination or reduction

- cost avoidance

- unit cost reduction

- new opportunities that can be taken advantage of

- reductions in elapsed time

- quality improvement in products or services

- improvement of quality of work life

- competitive advantage

In evaluating cost-justifications or quality improvements, it's important to realize that, even in the smallest companies, every white collar department is a customer of, or a supplier to, some other white collar department. Small gains in each department can add up to major competitive gains. And these gains increase geometrically when computers used for desktop publishing operate on networks which speed communication among individuals and workgroups.

Desktop publishing and network communication appear to be essential components of the long-heralded "office of the future." They have nothing to do with "office automation" — a notion which was quite reasonably feared and resisted by nearly all office workers. Instead, desktop publishing turns out to be a welcome tool for today's knowledge workers. Employees find preparing higher-quality products with desktop publishing rewarding. Employers find that desktop publishing produces higher-quality products, a more competitive work force, and an improved cost structure.

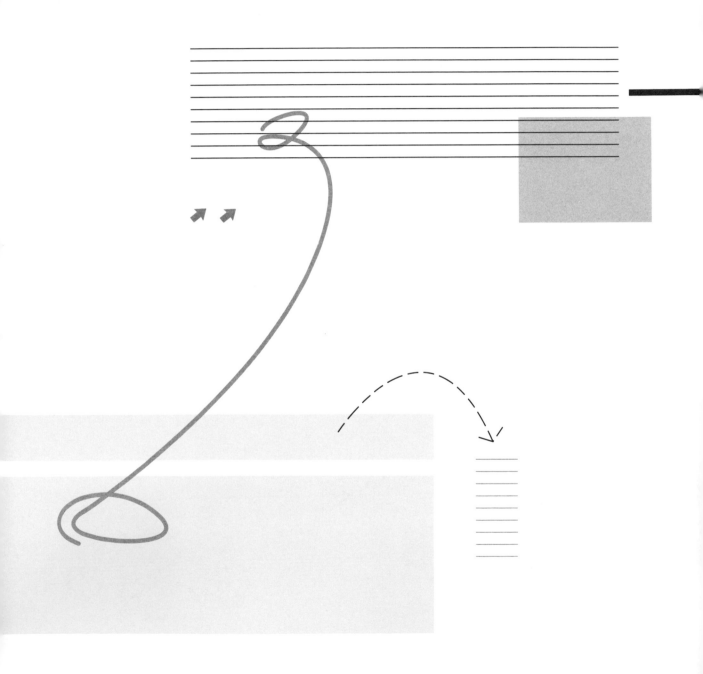

Reference

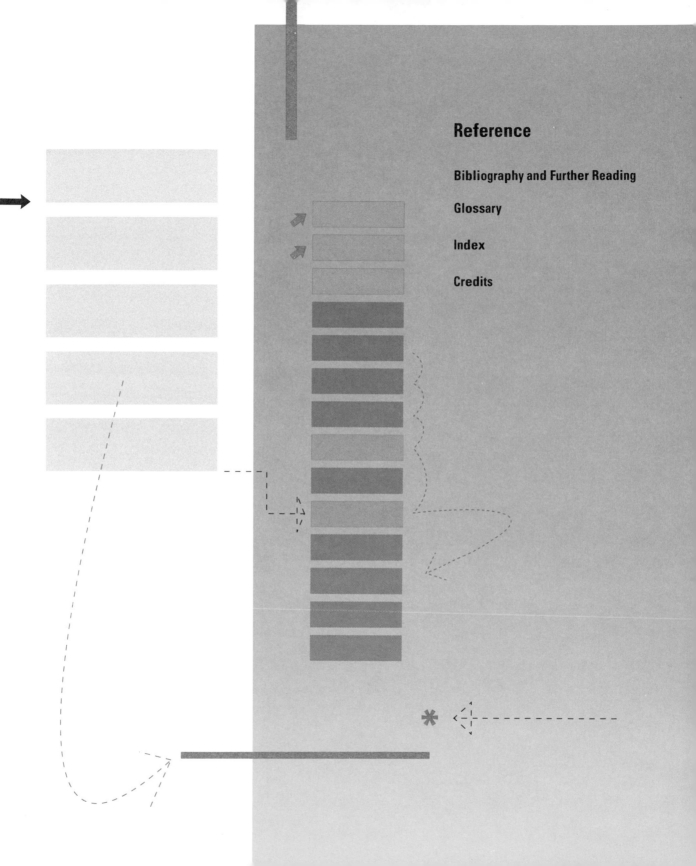

Bibliography and Further Reading

The one essential publication for anyone involved in publishing of any kind is The Chicago Manual of Style. *Most people involved in the graphic arts own a copy of* Pocket Pal. *Personal computer and desktop publishing magazines are the best sources for current information on hardware and software; in addition, they frequently publish articles on type and layout. Following are some useful books which were consulted in preparing this book.*

Beale, Stephen, and James Cavuoto. *The Scanner Book: A Complete Guide to the Use and Applications of Desktop Scanners*. Torrance, California: Micro Publishing Press, 1989.

Berenson, Conrad, and Raymond R. Colton. *Research and Report Writing for Business and Economics*. New York: Random House, 1971.

Bertin, Jacques. *Semiology of Graphics: Diagrams, Networks, Maps*. Translated by William J. Berg. Madison: Univ. of Wisconsin Press, 1983.

Birren, Faber, ed. *A Grammar of Color: A Basic Treatise on the Color System of Albert H. Munsell*. New York: Van Nostrand Reinhold Company, 1969.

Bureau, William H. *What the Printer Should Know About Paper*. Pittsburgh: Graphic Arts Technical Foundation, 1982.

Carter, Rob, Ben Day, and Philip Meggs. *Typographic Design: Form and Communication*. New York: Van Nostrand Reinhold Company, 1985.

Chappell, Warren. *A Short History of the Printed Word*. New York: Alfred A. Knopf, 1970.

The Chicago Manual of Style. Chicago: Univ. of Chicago Press, 1982. The most indispensable book in this list.

Craig, James. *Designing with Type: A Basic Course in Typography*. New York: Watson-Guptill Publications, 1971.

———. *Production for the Graphic Designer*. New York: Watson-Guptill Publications, 1974.

———, and Bruce Barton. *Thirty Centuries of Graphic Design*. New York: Watson-Guptill Publications, 1987.

Davis, Frederic E., John A. Barry, and Michael Wiesenberg. *Desktop Publishing*. Homewood, Illinois: Dow Jones-Irwin, 1986.

Felici, James, and Ted Nace. *Desktop Publishing Skills: A Primer for Typesetting with Computers and Laser Printers.* Reading, Pennsylvania: Addison-Wesley Publishing Company, 1987.

Frutiger, Adrian. *Type Sign Symbol.* Zurich: ABC Verlag, 1980.

Gray, Bill. *Studio Tips for Artists & Graphic Designers.* New York: Van Nostrand Reinhold Company, 1976.

————. *Tips on Type.* New York: Van Nostrand Reinhold Company, 1983.

Hunter, Dard. *Papermaking: The History and Technique of an Ancient Craft.* New York: Dover Publications, 1974.

International Paper Company. *Pocket Pal: A Graphic Arts Production Handbook.* New York: International Paper Company, 1989. A classic, first published in 1934. Updated most recently by Michael Bruno and Frank Romano. One of the great book bargains.

Kleper, Michael L. *The Illustrated Handbook of Desktop Publishing and Typesetting.* Blue Ridge Summit, Pennsylvania: TAB Professional and Reference Books, 1987.

Labuz, Ronald. *Typography & Typesetting.* New York: Van Nostrand Reinhold Company, 1988.

McClelland, Deke, and Craig Danuloff. *Desktop Publishing Type & Graphics: A Comprehensive Handbook.* New York: Harcourt Brace Jovanovich, 1987.

Meggs, Philip B. *A History of Graphic Design.* New York: Van Nostrand Reinhold Company, 1983.

Miles, John. *Design for Desktop Publishing: A Guide to Layout and Typography on the Personal Computer.* San Francisco: Chronicle Books, 1987.

Müller-Brockmann, Josef. *Grid Systems in Graphic Design: A Visual Communication Manual for Graphic Designers, Typographers and Three Dimensional Designers.* Niederteufen, Switzerland: Arthur Niggli, 1981.

Paper Corporation of America. *Dictionary of Graphic Arts Terms.* Wayne, Pennsylvania: Paper Corporation of America, 1986.

Parker, Roger C. *Looking Good in Print: A Guide to Basic Design for Desktop Publishing.* Chapel Hill, North Carolina: Ventana Press, 1988. A first-rate basic graphic design book.

Price, Jonathan, and Carlene Schnabel. *Desktop Publishing*. New York: Ballantine Books, 1987.

Romano, Frank J. *Desktop Typography with QuarkXPress*. Blue Ridge Summit, Pennsylvania: Windcrest Books, 1989.

———. *The TypEncyclopedia: A User's Guide to Better Typography*. New York: R. R. Bowker Company, 1984. Practical, straightforward and informative.

Rosen, Ben. *Type and Typography: The Designer's Type Book*, Revised Ed. New York: Van Nostrand Reinhold Company, 1976.

Saltman, David. *Paper Basics: Forestry, Manufacture, Selection, Purchasing, Mathematics and Metrics, Recycling*. New York: Van Nostrand Reinhold Company, 1978.

Sanders, Norman. *Graphic Designer's Production Handbook*. New York: Hastings House Publishers, 1982.

Seybold, John, and Fritz Dressler. *Publishing from the Desktop*. New York: Bantam Books, Inc., 1987. Very strong on computer and typesetting basics.

Skillin, Marjorie E., and Robert M. Gay. *Words into Type,* Third Ed. Englewood Cliffs, New Jersey: Prentice-Hall, 1974.

Stockford, James, ed. *Desktop Publishing Bible*. Indianapolis: Howard W. Sams & Company, 1987.

Stockton, James. *Designer's Guide to Color*. San Francisco: Chronicle Books, 1984.

Strunk, William, Jr., and E. B. White. *The Elements of Style*. New York: MacMillan, 1979.

Tufte, Edward. *The Visual Display of Quantitative Information*. Cheshire, Connecticut: Graphics Press, 1983.

White, Jan. *The Grid Book: A Guide to Page Planning*. Paramus, New Jersey: Graphic Design Software, Letraset U.S.A., 1987.

Xerox Corporation. *Helpful Facts About Paper*. Publication #610P500497. El Segundo, California, 1988.

Glossary

alkaline paper Paper formed in an acid-free process; long lasting, does not yellow with age.

antique finish Rough paper finish common in book and cover papers; handmade papers.

apostrophe In typography, a flying comma (').

application program Program used to manipulate information. Other kinds of programs, such as compilers and interpreters, mediate between the application software and the computer hardware.

artwork Any graphic element in a printing job, including photographs, charts, drawings.

ascender Stroke of a lowercase letter that extends above the x-height.

ASCII American Standard Code for Information Interchange, standard numbering scheme for characters and control commands. 0–32 represent nonprinting control commands; 33–127 represent the standard keyboard characters; 128–256 are used for different purposes by different systems.

auto Default linespacing of computer fonts, usually 120% of the body size, i.e., default linespacing for 10 pt type is usually 12 points (10/12).

back up To print the back side of a sheet already printed on the front.

bad break Poor hyphenation, or starting a column with a widow or a hyphenated syllable such as "-ing."

baseline Line on which type characters sit, below which descenders descend.

basis weight Measurement of paper's weight versus surface area. It is the weight in pounds of one ream of paper (500 sheets) cut in a grade's basic size (which varies from grade to grade).

baud Rate of telecommunication transmission (usually 1200, 2400, or 9600 bits per second).

benday Method of laying a screen (dots, lines, other textures) on artwork or plates to obtain various tones and shadings.

binding Transforming printed sheets into folders, booklets, or books. Usually includes collating, scoring, folding, stitching or gluing, and trimming.

bit map Electronic representation of a page, indicating the position of every possible spot. 300 dpi printing devices have 300 dots (spots) per linear inch (90,000 dots/square in); 1270 dpi devices have 1.6 million dots/square inch.

bit Binary digit, the smallest possible unit of information, on-or-off, one-or-zero, plus-or-minus.

blanket In offset lithography, the rubber-surfaced roller which transfers the image from plate to paper.

bleed Any part of the printed image that extends to the trim edge of the page. A bleed can also go across the gutter.

blueprint, blueline In offset lithography, a photo-print made from the negatives that will be used to make the printing plate. It serves as a final proof, folded and assembled to show how the final job will print.

body size (of type) Vertical measurement of type plus surrounding space (leading); 9/12 indicates 9 pt letterforms on 12 pt bodies.

bold, boldface Heavyweight type used for emphasis. The type distinguishing the words defined in this glossary is **bold**.

bond paper Strong, durable paper used for letterheads, laser printing, and other business purposes. May be made from cotton fiber, wood pulp, or a combination. May be watermarked.

border Printed line or design around artwork.

brightness Ability of paper to reflect light.

bristol (board) Stiff, heavyweight paper suitable for covers, menus, cards.

bullet Typographic dot or other pointer used to set off items in lists.

byte A set of 8 computer bits.

C1S Paper or cover stock coated on one side.

C2S Paper or cover stock coated on both sides.

calender To smooth the surface of paper with polished rollers.

caliper Thickness of paper, measured in *points* (thousandths of an inch, not typographers' points.

callout Identifying words associated with a picture, often connected by a leader line. Sometimes used as a synonym for *pull quote*, words extracted from text and set in display type.

camera-ready Ready to be photographed by the printer.

cap height Height of capital letters in a typeface.

caption Explanatory information for a graphic.

character Any letter of the alphabet, numeral, punctuation mark, space, or other typeset symbol.

chemical pulp Wood pulp in which the cellulose fibers have been separated chemically under heat and pressure. Fine papers are made from chemical pulp; newsprint is made from the alternative, *groundwood* (*mechanical*) pulp.

chroma Color intensity.

clip art Illustrations and designs collected and sold commercially.

coated free sheet Glossy paper which contains less than 25% groundwood pulp.

coated papers Papers coated with clay and other substances to provide an enamel surface for high reflectance, good ink coverage, and sharp printed images.

collate Assemble pages and sections of a booklet for binding.

colophon Description of the typefaces and production methods used in a book.

color break(s) Artwork prepared so as to indicate which elements print in which ink color. Copy and art for each color may be pasted on separate boards, on overlays, or color may be indicated in pencil on an overlay sheet of tissue paper.

color separation Photographing or scanning color artwork for process printing through filters to separate colors for each of the process inks to be used.

column head Heading of a table identifying the entries in the column directly below. A heading covering more than one column is called a *spanner*.

composition Assembly and arrangement of typeset characters into words, lines, and paragraphs.

comprehensive ("comp") A visualization of a design. May be "loose" or "tight" — depending on whether it's a rough sketch or closely resembles the final printed job.

continuous-tone Made up of innumerable shades and tints which blend into one another. Applies to artwork such as photographs, oil paintings, watercolors.

copier paper Commonly 20 lb bond paper designed to be printed xerographically; may be high-speed or multi-purpose.

copy Generic term sometimes used to indicate text, sometimes used to mean all camera-ready material.

CPU Central processing unit of a computer.

cropping Selecting a portion of an image for printing.

CRT Cathode ray tube. Any TV-like raster device.

curl Distortion of paper caused by reaction to environmental conditions. Can cause feeding problems in a press or electronic printer. The *curl side* is the concave side.

curly quotation mark See *quotation marks*.

cyan Process blue printing ink.

dandy roll Cylinder on a paper machine for creating finishes, such as wove, laid, or linen, and for adding watermarks.

deck One line of a headline. Sometimes a smaller second headline is called a *deck head* or *drop head*.

deckle Irregular-edged text/cover paper made in multiple plies. Used for announcements, high-quality booklets.

descender Stroke of a lowercase letter extending below the baseline.

digitize Convert information to computer-readable form. Digitized typesetting is the creation of typographic characters by the arrangement of black and white spots called *pixels*.

dimensional stability Degree to which paper maintains its size and shape in the printing process and when subjected to changes in moisture content or relative humidity.

dingbat Decorative character, such as: ☞○✳✏.

disk Magnetic medium on which a computer stores information. Can be a large-capacity hard disk or an easily transportable floppy disk.

display type Type set larger than the text to attract attention.

document Computer file created with an application program.

dot Smallest mark a laser printer makes (a better term is *spot*). Also, a cell of a halftone screen, which may be expressed as a percentage of the cell filled with ink, as in a *50% dot*.

driver Program that translates instructions from an application program into a form that can be understood by a printer.

dull-coated (dull finish) Smooth coated paper, low in gloss.

dummy Blank version of a book or booklet made from the paper stocks specified in order to demonstrate binding, weight, and size of the finished item.

duotone Halftone image rendered in two dot colors, one of which is usually black.

electronic printing Any technology that reproduces pages without the use of traditional ink, water, or chemistry. Usually electrostatic or electrophotographic.

electrostatic printing or copying Printing process which works by creating an image with an electrostatic charge on a polished plate, attracting magnetic ink (toner) to the plate, and transferring it to paper with heat and pressure.

em Unit of space (width) equal to the point size of the type.

emboss To stamp a raised or depressed area or image into paper with metal dies after printing.

en Half an em.

engrave Produce a raised printed surface by printing with a cutaway plate.

file Any collection of information stored on a disk — application program, document, directory, etc.

finish Surface property of (usually uncoated) paper. Most common are vellum, wove, lustre, antique, laid, linen.

flat Film negatives arranged (*stripped-up*) for making printing plates.

flush In typography, "even with."

flying comma See *quotation marks.*

foldout Extra page that may be pasted or folded into a book or booklet.

folio A page number or a numbered page.

font Typeface. May refer to a family (e.g., *Helvetica*), weight (e.g., *light*), style (e.g., *italic*), and/or width (e.g., *condensed*).

front end system Workstation or group of workstations containing the application's software for preparing pages of type and graphics.

fountain solution Solution of water, gum arabic, and various types of etches, used to repel ink from non-printing areas of the lithographic plate.

fraction bar Diagonal slash shorter than a solidus.

gatefold Four-page insert or cover with foldouts on either side, making the equivalent of 8 pages.

grain In paper, the direction in which fibers line up.

grayscale Range of intensity increments between white and black.

gripper Part of the press or printer that holds the paper and guides it through the press; the edge of the paper so held.

groundwood Pulp made by mechanically grinding wood to separate the cellulose fibers. Groundwood pulp is used in less expensive papers, such as newsprint, where less strength and brightness are required and lower cost is important.

gutter Space between columns of type; the place where pages meet in a book or booklet.

halftone Reproduction of continuous-tone art as a picture formed by dots of various sizes.

halftone screen Engraved glass for turning continuous-tone artwork into halftone dots. The fineness of the screen is specified by number of dots or lines per inch: the higher the number, the higher the quality of the printed image.

hang Place characters outside the left margin.

holdout Ability of a paper to hold ink on the surface instead of absorbing it. Papers with good holdout produce sharper printed images.

hue Color name (*yellow, blue, green, etc.*).

hyphenation and justification (h&j) Filling out type lines of fixed width with extra space (usually wordspace) and hyphens. Hyphenation can also be used to even out line width in ragged right composition.

imagesetter Electronic device that outputs type, line art, and photos. Generally refers to high-resolution output on photo paper or film. Sometimes called *typesetting*, but a typesetter outputs type only.

imposition Arrangement of pages for printing so that they will be in correct order when the sheet is folded.

impression cylinder Cylinder of an offset press that squeezes the paper against the blanket cylinder carrying the image.

indention Style for the first line of a paragraph. There are three kinds: *left* or *hanging* (sometimes called *outdenting*), no indention (but with extra space to signal next paragraph), and *right*.

index Of paper, a strong, heavyweight bristol. Also, a pi character used for pointing (☞).

indicia Printed mailing permit markings.

inkjet printer Printer that sprays ink onto paper through computer-controlled nozzles.

italic Font or style where the letters slant. Used for emphasis.

kern Tighten letterspace for better optical appearance of pairs of letters such as *AY* and *Yo*.

kilobyte 1024 bytes (a thousand).

kraft Extremely strong paper used when durability is important. May be unbleached and brown like a grocery bag, bleached, or bleached and dyed, as in the case of gray kraft envelopes.

laid Ribbed paper finish. Molds used for the earliest paper imparted this finish, hence laid paper is the closest in appearance to handmade paper.

laser paper Smooth, bright, heavyweight paper designed to produce maximum image resolution when printed on laser printers. Smoothness results in even toner coverage; brightness produces high-contrast images.

laser printer Electrostatic printer which uses laser beams to create the image area. A polished selenium drum acts as the printing plate.

leading Extra space between lines of type.

leader Row of dashes or dots to lead the eye across a column.

leaf Page with printing on both sides. Each side is a *folio*.

letterspacing Extra space between letters.

ligature In a typeface, two or more letters merged into one, as in fi and fl.

line art Artwork in which all marks are individual strokes. Examples are pen-and-ink drawings, engravings, and woodcuts.

line A row of type. In typography, a straight line is called a *rule*.

linespacing Distance from baseline to baseline.

lint Particles of paper dust, which degrade print quality.

lithography Printing process where image areas and non-image areas are separated chemically.

local area network (LAN) A group of workstations, storage units (file servers), printout devices (print servers), communications devices, and printers linked by wire or cable for simultaneous high-speed communication.

logotype Special typographic treatment of a name, usually that of an organization. May include a special symbol.

lowercase "Small" letters.

M weight Weight of 1,000 sheets cut to a specific size. Useful because paper is usually priced by the pound.

magenta Process red printing ink.

matte finish Non-glossy, but smooth, paper finish.

measure Width in picas.

mechanical boards Also called *boards, paste-ups, keylines*. Camera-ready assembly of type, graphics, and instructions for the printer pasted on illustration board with registration marks for alignment when printing more than one color.

mechanical separations Overlays on mechanical boards made to indicate position of each separate color.

megabyte 1,024 kilobytes (one million bytes).

menu Method for selecting from a list of options on a computer screen. Selection is by mouse pointer or keystrokes.

modem Telephone line interface between computers.

moiré Undesirable interference patterns caused by misalignment of halftone screens.

multilith Small duplicating offset press.

negative letterspacing Subtraction of inter-character space, either between specific pairs (kerning) or *en masse* (tight tracking).

offset lithography Most common commercial printing process, in which the ink is offset from the plate to a rubber blanket cylinder before being transferred to paper.

oldstyle numerals Numerals in which the body sits on the baseline so that there are ascenders and descenders. Used in text but not in tabular work.

one-up, two-up, three-up, etc. Number of units of a publication printed at one time.

opacity Property of paper that prevents showthrough from one side to another.

orphan First line of a paragraph that falls at the bottom of a page or column.

out-of-register Out-of-focus multicolor printing caused by misalignment of printing plates.

page description language (PDL) Powerful computer program that converts text and formatting created with an application program into bit-mapping instructions for a laser printer or other output device.

page One side of a *leaf*. Pages, also called *folios*, are either odd-numbered right-hand pages (*recto*) or even-numbered left-hand pages (*verso*).

paste-up Type and graphics pasted in exact position on a piece of illustration board to be photographed by the printer. Also called a *mechanical*.

perfecting Printing the back of a sheet already printed on one side.

peripheral Hardware such as a disk drive, printer, or modem, used under a computer's control. Usually connected by cable or wire.

photostat High-resolution photocopy reproduced on photopaper.

pi Non-standard type characters, such as map symbols, arrows, boxes and bullets. A popular pi font is *Zapf Dingbats*.

pica Typographic unit of measure equal to 12 points.

picking The pulling off of particles from a paper's surface during printing. Particles accumulate on the plate or blanket, causing *hickies* and other printing defects.

pixel Picture element, the basic unit of digital imaging. Represents the presence or absence of a spot (zero or one).

plate cylinder Cylinder on a rotary press to which the metal printing plate is attached.

platemaking Process of exposing and developing the photochemical plate used to transfer the image on an offset press.

point Smallest unit of typographic measure, 1/72 of an inch. Used to specify the height of type and the distance between lines. Abbreviation: *pt* (no period required).

pre-press Tasks usually handled by the printer prior to printing, such as color separation, stripping, and platemaking.

primary colors The three basic colors of ink — red, yellow, and blue — from which all others are mixed. *Additive primaries* are the three basic colors of *light* corresponding to receptors in the eye: red, blue, green. *Subtractive primaries* are magenta (red-blue), yellow (red-green), and cyan (blue-green).

prime Typewriter apostrophe ('). Also, *double prime* ("). Properly used to designate feet and inches, but not apostrophes and quotation marks.

printer font Collection of bit-mapped characters which can be interpreted by a page description language and drawn to scale by a laser printer.

process inks Cyan, yellow, magenta, and black inks used in process printing.

process printing Printing from several halftone plates (usually four or more) with process inks (cyan, yellow, magenta, black) to produce intermediate colors and the effect of continuous-tone color.

pulp Beaten and refined vegetable fibers (cellulose) to which chemicals and fillers are added, used to make paper.

quotation marks Single or double *inverted* and *flying commas* (' ' " "). Should be distinguished from *primes* (' ").

rag paper Paper containing at least 25% rag or cotton fiber pulp.

ragged Typesetting style where lines are of uneven length, usually flush left, ragged right.

RAM (random access memory) Part of the computer memory that stores information temporarily while it is in use.

raster Grid on which an image is produced.

raster image processor (RIP) Controller that creates an image by drawing it on a grid with a moving beam (like a laser beam), which is turned on and off according to coded instructions. In the case of laser printers, these instructions are written in page description language. The result is a high-resolution bit map built up of very small dots.

RC paper Resin-coated photopaper used in high-resolution type-setting.

ream 500 sheets of paper.

recto Right-hand page (odd-numbered).

reflective copy Artwork such as a photograph or painting that will be photographed by the printer using reflected light. Alternatives are film positives (slides) or negatives.

register mark Reference mark, usually a cross in a circle, applied to mechanicals before photography, to achieve alignment where there are overlays or color separations.

repro Type proofs, usually on RC paper.

reprographic paper Copier paper.

resolution Quantification of printout quality using the number of spots (or dots) per inch.

reverse Type appearing in white or a color on black. Sometimes called *knockout* or *dropout* if the printed image is dark and the type is the color of the paper.

river Unsightly white space running down a column of type.

ROM (read only memory) The part of memory that contains information the computer uses repeatedly.

roman Font or style where the letters are plain, i.e., not italic or bold.

roughs Loosely sketched graphic design ideas, usually in colored pencil on tracing paper, developing several approaches.

rubylith Two-layer acetate film of red or amber emulsion on a clear base for making color separations.

rule Vertical or horizontal typographic line.

run-in head A subhead, usually in bold or italic type, which is part of a paragraph.

runaround Type that flows around a picture (either the frame or the picture itself).

runnability Paper qualities related to strength, dimensional stability, cleanliness and surface integrity that determine how well a sheet performs on press.

running header, footer Headline at the top or bottom of every page (e.g., main title on the top of each right-hand page, chapter title on each left, page numbers and date at the bottom).

saddle stitch Simple, inexpensive binding method using staples at the fold.

sans serif Typeface without serifs.

scaling Resizing an image to be printed.

scanner An electronic device which converts an image into digital information. Scanners are used for color separation and for reading text and graphics into computers.

score Crease with a dull rule in preparation for folding.

screen font Computer program containing instructions needed by the computer to draw letterforms on the screen and other information, such as kerning pair tables.

screen ruling Lines or dots per inch of a halftone screen.

serif Short lines or flourishes projecting from the main strokes of type letterforms. Serifs are thought to improve readability by directing the eye horizontally.

set solid Type set without extra space between lines (e.g., 10/10). This is not the same as the automatic specification of desktop fonts, which usually have about 20% extra linespace.

shade Degree of whiteness or blackness of a color.

signature Folded press sheet consisting of 4, 8, 12, 16, or 32 pages.

sinkage Extra white space at the top of a page, usually for a title page or the first page of a chapter.

slitter Machine for cutting rolls of paper lengthwise. Source of slitter dust, which can contaminate the printing.

small caps Capital letters close in size to the lowercase letters of the typeface. Good for long passages in caps or as an emphatic alternative to boldface and italic. Standard for A.M. and P.M., and *A.D.* and *B.C.*

smoothness Flatness of a sheet of paper, which affects resolution of printed image.

solidus Diagonal slash or *virgule* (/).

spanner In a table, column head that has subsidiary column heads under it.

spiral binding Mechanical binding using a single wire passing through pre-drilled holes.

spot The smallest mark that can be made by an output device — such as a laser printer — which is controlled by a raster image processor.

spot color Color used in type and line work for emphasis (c.f. *process color*).

spread Facing pages.

stripping Assembling film negatives into *flats* for platemaking.

stub Left-hand column of a table.

style sheet Set of typographic specifications for components of a document, such as headlines, subheads, normal text, footnotes, tables, etc.

style Variation of a typeface, such as bold or italic.

substance Basis weight of certain grades of paper. (20 lb bond is also called *substance 20*, or *sub 20*.)

surprint To print one color of ink on top of another.

text paper Very high-quality paper made in white and colors, in many textures and weights. Many have matching cover sheets.

thermography Printing process in which an engraved look is achieved by fusing thick ink to paper. It is not a good idea to run thermographed paper (stationery, for example) through a laser printer, because the heat generated by the printer may melt the inks.

thumbnail Rough sketch of a layout.

tissue overlay Sheet of tissue paper on a piece of artwork or a mechanical with instructions to the printer, including color indications.

toner Plastic magnetic ink used in electronic printing.

transparency (chrome) Film color positive, such as a 35mm slide.

trap Overlap allowed when two colors print adjacent to one another. Used to avoid a white space between the two colors.

trim To cut away folded or uneven edges; the final size of a printed piece.

typography The choice and arrangement of type.

uncoated offset papers Good quality, general-purpose, uncoated printing papers.

uppercase Capital letters.

verso Left-hand page (even-numbered).

virgule Diagonal slash, *solidus* (/).

watermark Non-functional design impressed on paper during manufacture. Usually for letterheads.

widow Short last line of a paragraph which appears as the first line of a page or column. Also, a word by itself in the last line of a paragraph.

wire-o binding Elegant mechanical binding using double series of wire loops through slots rather than holes.

wove Smooth paper finish.

wysiwyg Acronym for "what you see is what you get," indicating that the typographic page viewed on the screen of a workstation essentially represents what the printer will output.

x-height Height of the lowercase letter *x*, an important characteristic in distinguishing typefaces.

xerography Electrostatic printing using magnetic ink particles (toner) where the image is fused to the paper by heat and pressure.

Source Notes

Listed below are sources for copyrighted materials. A number of historical illustrations in 2.3 and 4.2 are in the public domain. All other original page designs, illustrations, and photographs were produced by Business Information Graphics, Inc.

Page   6   Xerographic printer diagram reprinted from The Waite Group's *Desktop Publishing Bible*, edited by James Stockford, published by Howard W. Sams & Company, © 1987 by The Waite Group. Reprinted with permission.

7   Illustration of how color printers work adapted from Ron Risley, "Printing a Rainbow," *Macworld*, vol. 6, no. 1 (January, 1989), 136–37.

8   Diagram of digital printing press adapted from prospectus of Presstek, Inc., March 28, 1989.

14   Letterforms illustration courtesy of Bitstream Inc., Cambridge, MA.

15   Ventura illustrations courtesy of Electronic Directions, New York.

25   Top template illustration is from Aldus® Corporation's PageMaker Portfolio™. Used with the express permission of Aldus Corporation. PageMaker Portfolio is a trademark of Aldus Corporation.

Bottom template illustration courtesy of Quark, Inc., Denver, CO.

26   IBM 1976 Annual Report courtesy of International Business Machines Corporation.

"Inner City Infill," a poster announcing a competition for architects to design urban housing, was designed by Michael Bierut, Vignelli Associates, for the New York State Council on the Arts.

"One Color/Two Color" poster was designed by Michael Mabry, Michael Mabry Design, San Francisco, CA, for the American Institute of Graphic Arts.

29   Johann Gutenberg portrait courtesy of The New York Public Library; The Rare Books and Manuscripts Division; Astor, Lenox, and Tilden Foundations.

30   Aldus Manutius portrait courtesy of The New York Public Library; The Rare Books and Manuscripts Division; Astor, Lenox, and Tilden Foundations.

Bembo and Garamond courtesy of Monotype Typography, Woburn, MA.

31   Giambattista Bodoni portrait courtesy of The New York Public Library; The Rare Books and Manuscripts Division; Astor, Lenox, and Tilden Foundations.

Bodoni Book courtesy of Monotype Typography, Woburn, MA.

Detail from *Napoleon in His Study*, Jacques-Louis David, courtesy of the National Gallery of Art, Washington, DC, Samuel H. Kress Collection.

32   Photograph of Paul Renner courtesy of Linotype Company, Hauppauge, NY.

Cartoon and *Too Much* typefaces courtesy of Image Club Graphics, Inc., Calgary, Alberta, Canada.

Page 40   Seashell graphic courtesy of GoldMind Publishing, Riverside, CA, from MacGraphics (3.0) Collection. (Also appears on page 70.)

71   Flip chart courtesy of Greenwich Asset Management, Greenwich, CT.

89   The graphs were produced by SYGRAPH, a statistical and scientific graphics software program published by SYSTAT, Inc., Evanston, IL.

90   Clip art courtesy of T/Maker Company, Mountain View, CA, © 1988, all rights reserved. From the ClickArt EPS Illustrations Portfolio.

101   Top photograph courtesy of Hewlett-Packard Company.

Bottom photograph courtesy of Iris Graphics, Inc., Bedford, MA.

102   Color printer output of the frog courtesy of Tektronix, Inc., Wilsonville, OR.

107   Color charts adapted from James Stockton, *Designer's Guide to Color 2* San Francisco, Chronicle Books, 1984.

127   Henri de Toulouse-Lautrec, Cover No. 1 of *L'Estampe Originale*, 1893. Color lithograph, 17¾" x 23¾", The Metropolitan Museum of Art, New York, Rogers Fund, 1922.

128   Diagram adapted from *Production for the Graphic Designer* by James Craig, © 1974 by Watson-Guptill Publications, New York.

Photographs courtesy of Heidelberg Eastern, Inc.

130   Diagram adapted from *Production for the Graphic Designer* by James Craig, © 1974 by Watson-Guptill Publications, New York.

140   Illustrations reprinted from *Production for the Graphic Designer* by James Craig, © 1974 by Watson-Guptill Publications, New York. Reprinted with permission.

143   Photographs, Hammermill Papers, International Paper.

149   Photographs, Hammermill Papers, International Paper.

151   Watermarks courtesy of The New York Public Library, Picture Collection, The Branch Libraries.

166   Flip chart courtesy of Greenwich Asset Management, Greenwich, CT.

Photograph courtesy of Eastman Kodak Company, Rochester, NY.

167   Photograph of Barcodata 600 projector courtesy of BARCO, Inc., Atlanta, GA, manufacturers of large-screen projection equipment.

173   Slides courtesy of Microsoft PowerPoint.

Index

Technical terms are defined in the Glossary, which is not indexed here.

Notices

Desktop Papers, Laser Print, Laser Plus, Hammermill Bond, and Hammermill Offset Opaque are trademarks of International Paper Company.

Adobe and PostScript are registered trademarks, and Carta is a trademark of Adobe Systems Incorporated.

PageMaker is a registered trademark of Aldus Corporation.

Apple and LaserWriter are registered trademarks, and Macintosh is a trademark of Apple Computer, Inc.

Autologic is a trademark of Autologic, Inc.

CompuServe is a registered trademark of CompuServe Corp.

Dow Jones News/Retrieval is a registered trademark of Dow Jones & Company, Inc.

Futura is a registered trademark of Fundicion Tipografica Neufville S.A.

Heidelberg GTO and Heidelberg Speedmaster are trademarks of Heidelberg Eastern, Inc.

IBM is a registered trademark of International Business Machines Corporation.

ITC New Baskerville and ITC Zapf Dingbats are registered trademarks of International Typeface Corporation.

Franklin Gothic is a registered trademark of Kingsley/ATF Type Corporation.

Helvetica, Univers, Times, Janson Text, and Palatino are registered trademarks, and Linotronic is a trademark of Linotype AG and/or its subsidiaries.

Microsoft, Microsoft Word, PowerPoint, and MS-DOS are registered trademarks of Microsoft Corporation.

Monotype, Monotype Garamond, Bembo, and Century Schoolbook are registered trademarks of The Monotype Corporation plc.

MacSlab, Railway, and Neuland are trademarks of NeoScribe International.

Xerox and Ventura Publisher are trademarks of Xerox Corporation.

Other brand or product names are trademarks or registered trademarks of their respective holders.

This book was created using standard desktop computers and software. Imagesetting was done by Axiom Design Systems, New York. It was printed on 80 lb Hammermill Offset Opaque, Lustre Finish, at Daniels Printing Company, Boston.

Design: Business Information Graphics, Inc., New York
         Ilene Korey Price

Comments

Comments and suggestions about *The Hammermill Guide to Desktop Publishing in Business* should be addressed to:

Guide to Desktop Publishing
Hammermill Papers
6400 Poplar Avenue
Memphis, TN 38197

Additional Copies

To order *The Hammermill Guide to Desktop Publishing in Business,* telephone 1-800-242-2148. Major credit cards accepted.

Paper Samples

For free sample packets of Hammermill Desktop Papers® and the name of your nearest supplier, call 1-800-242-2148.